DOING
CHILD AND
ADOLESCENT
PSYCHOTHERAPY

DOING CHILD AND ADOLESCENT PSYCHOTHERAPY
The Ways and Whys

RICHARD BROMFIELD, PH.D.

JASON ARONSON INC.
Northvale, New Jersey
London

Production Editor: Elaine Lindenblatt

This book was set in 12pt. Bembo by Alpha Graphics of Pittsfield, NH and printed and bound by Book-mart Press, Inc. of North Bergen, NJ.

Library of Congress Cataloging-in-Publication Data

Bromfield, Richard.
   Doing child and adolescent psychotherapy : the ways and whys /
Richard Bromfield.
      p. cm.
   Includes bibliographical references and index.
   ISBN 0-7657-0220-7
   1. Child psychotherapy. 2. Adolescent psychotherapy. 3. Play
therapy. I. Title.
   RJ504.B753 1999
   618.92'8914—dc21   99-12391

Printed in the United States of America on acid-free paper. For information and catalog write to Jason Aronson Inc., 230 Livingston Street, Northvale, NJ 07647-1726, or visit our website: www.aronson.com

Contents

III. THE REST

Preface

We child therapists need no convincing of the seriousness and arduousness of our mission. In our most splendid moments we see our young patients heal and go forth on solid ground toward happier and more satisfying lives. At other and more usual times we help children and their parents get through another day or week with less mishap and destruction or, perhaps, leave our offices with a little less pain and suffering than when they came. And sadly, there are the darkest times, when our best efforts do not help at all.

Our purpose is not, as some observers think, simply to be a friend or confidant to the child. That would be easy. As I've written elsewhere (Bromfield 1997), children's playing in therapy is much more than mere fun or pretend-to-be-taken seriously. What we do is complex, wearing, slow, and uncertain in its progress and outcome. And much of what we do we do alone—without help, confirmation, or encouragement, often against the odds or under disapproving eyes. Done properly, being a child therapist is hard and noble work.

This book is dedicated to that worthy and challenging purpose. With vivid clinical material and personal candor, the theoretical essence and practical essentials of doing child and adolescent psychotherapy are laid out, from the referral call to the last goodbye, capturing the intricacies and subtleties of children and their therapies in their biggest and smallest ways—and everywhere in between. Whatever aspect of therapy is discussed, our eyes and ears are aimed toward what is transpiring in the child, in the therapist, and in the space they share. And whatever the clinical situation being examined, a slow and steady focus on the building and meaning of relationships—between child and family, child and world, child and therapist, inner and outer experience—ever reigns supreme in these pages. The belief that the therapist's most powerful, if not sole, therapeutic tool is himself pervades every nook and cranny of the book and serves as its foundation.

I hope this intimate and pragmatic guide to child psychotherapy renews, fortifies, and enriches the important work you, as child therapist, pursue every moment of every clinical hour.

—RB

Acknowledgments

How does one thank the near-countless colleagues, supervisors, supervisees, and patients who have taught me hour by hour since I first walked in, on wobbly knees, to meet my first child in therapy? I hope those who have taught me best can see and hear themselves in these pages. Again, a knowing nod to M.C., with whom I, learning about myself, learned much about myself as a therapist, too. Last, my appreciation goes to my editor, Cindy Hyden, whose natural sensibility and respect for the preciousness of therapeutic process wholly resonated with the book's spirit, herding me when I or my writing strayed from that aspiration.

To the Reader

As I wrote previously, "I use *children* to mean children and adolescents of all ages. If I need to define a child or group more narrowly, I use other terms, such as infant, toddler, adolescent, or first-grader. I refer to those I see in therapy as *patients* (though I appreciate the sentiments of those preferring the term *clients*). When speaking about children or therapists in general, I randomly alternate male and female pronouns to avoid the intolerable monotony of he and she, her or him" (Bromfield 1997, p. 9).

I

THE
ESSENTIALS

1

EASY
DOES IT:
BEGINNING
THERAPY

Beginnings are important, arguably critical. A small misstep can detour us unnecessarily; a large enough one can derail the whole journey. At the very least, the first steps, the ones from which all other steps follow, are the foundations on which therapies, and the essential relationship within, are built.

We begin with the parents, because they are generally the ones who choose, arrange, and pay for a child's psychotherapy. Consider the challenge facing the mothers and fathers who call us. In a handful of minutes they try their best to present an enormously complicated, painful, and often embarrassing situation to a complete stranger who purports to be some kind of expert on matters of children and families. As former students we know how intellectually demanding case formulating can be. Imagine adding the heavy measure of worry, self-blame, and hopelessness that parents know.

Whatever their issues, we try to listen patiently. If we are rushed that day, we say so and offer a better time to talk in the near future. Sensitized to the difficulty of their call, we try to help parents tell their story—asking helpful questions of the timid, slowing the speedy, organizing the rambling. We do so not only to foster a connection, but to see what the problem is and whether it is one that we can help solve.

A few more moments on the phone might convince us that we are not the appropriate clinician, might inform our making an effective referral elsewhere. Or they could help us distinguish true crises from entitled demands or reveal the basic motive for the call to us (e.g., seeking not therapy for the child, but evidence with which to attack a spouse's sole custody). Such extra time is well spent on the first call and is in everyone's best interest. It preserves the clinician's time to do treatment. It saves the patient hours and money and, by helping get the child to the right help sooner, it saves on the emotional toll of premature investment in the wrong therapist.

When sensing a mismatch, we gently—so as to minimize any feelings of rejection—describe how children, particularly adolescents, tend to connect most with the therapist they see first. Meeting with us, we further explain, could obstruct connecting with a second therapist. For many parents and children meeting a therapist and sharing their stories is both draining and bonding. It is almost always best to save the powerful early meetings for the therapist of final destination (though sometimes clinical conditions or the restraints of health care systems require patients to see a series of practitioners en route to treatment).

While we are assessing matters, so are parents, who in many instances do their shopping for a therapist as we speak. What do patients look for? All sorts of things. Facts, such as what we do, what we charge, what kinds of insurance we accept, whether we have openings, where the office is.

Many parents have begun to form impressions of us even before hearing our voices. If we have come highly recommended, there may be halos around our heads. While inflated views of what we can do make for easier and enthusiastic beginnings, they can just as often backfire, leading to disappointment and impatience, even premature endings, when our work does not produce big enough or fast enough results.

Conversely, and more commonly in today's busy and tight marketplace, parents who actually prefer other therapists consult us because of insurance plan constraints or matters of distance or scheduling. To one disgruntled mother who saw me at best as her distant second choice, I said, "You've mentioned several times having to stick to a list of providers." Putting such dissatisfaction on the table helped her to speak her mind concerning her ultimate doubt as to whether any therapist could help. Sharing this thought with me gave her a bit more confidence in the process and led to her giving me a fair chance to prove myself with her and her daughter.

I see the purpose of the initial call as deciding whether future contact with me is likely to benefit the child. If it makes sense that we go no further, I aspire to give parents a good experience with me as representative of the mental health profession so that they will persist in their quest for help. And when we do agree to meet in person, this call has gotten us off on sure footing, the work well begun.

FIRST MEETINGS

With younger children, I typically offer parents the option of meeting with me first without their child. This provides an opportunity for the parents to speak freely and to check me out before bringing their child. I suggest that parents of elementary school children accompany their child. In contrast, I urge parents to let their teenage children come to the beginning hour by themselves, explaining that doing so counters the common adolescent tendency to mistrust and reject the therapist as just another arm of the parents' authority. I bend, however, to comply with parents' good reasons for other arrangements (e.g., a ninth-grade girl who fears going anywhere without her mother, or including a very young sibling who cannot be left alone in the waiting room). Regardless of the child's age, in the course of the initial meetings, I try to meet with both children and parents, alone and together. This early negotiating, structuring, and educating concerning who should come begins to show parents how their children and therapy work.

Making our patients feel safe—the absolute first requisite to any worthwhile course of therapy—begins in the earliest moments. Do we take a minute to greet everyone who has come with the child? Are we kindly? Do we smile sincerely? Do we look the child and his mother in the eye?

Or do we appear to be just doing a job, grudgingly serving the next customer? Do we ask how they're doing, then turn away and head into the office before they've answered? Five minutes of simple patience for a disorganized mother to gather her several children and their belongings may accomplish more than the official office time we salvage by rushing her. By themselves insufficient to ensure good treatment, these civilities—done in good measure, neither to feign sympathy nor to manipulate—convey a sense of us as real persons and help our patients make the transition to the world of therapy they are about to enter.

When we go out to meet new child patients, some zip past us like Speedy Gonzalez, rifling through our toy boxes, or even our desks, before we've said hello. A majority of them follow the lead of their parents, who follow ours. Others dally, coming at a snail's pace out of fear or to show who's boss.

Sure that I, at this point, can be sure of little, I tend to stay out of the line of fire. I let parents and child struggle their way into the office, reminding myself that they somehow manage their lives when I am not around. I do not force anyone to come in, for that is the quickest way to nowhere. My threats or tugs may get a reluctant child inside today, but there's a good chance he won't return tomorrow. And should the child return, she will see me as someone to be mistrusted, someone who has little respect for what she wants and does. Frustrating as it is, seldom in a treatment can we hurry what must come in its own time.

I can't recall a single instance when I have denied a child's wish to come in either with or without someone. Soon after settling in, however, I turn our attention to the reasons for such demands, leading to a readjusting of who should and shouldn't be there. While I do not force a child to separate from a parent against her will, I do bring to the foreground the desperate nature of her fear, a fear that will quickly take center stage in her therapy.

When parents cannot get a child out of the car to even come to the waiting room, I—once establishing that the child is physically safe in the car—spend my time consulting with them, helping them to better understand and manage their child. Anything but a waste, such sessions prove to be at least as valuable as if the child had come voluntarily (which usually happens the following week).

Once in my office, I say hello again. Children seem to appreciate this and sense that, under their parents' and my watchful eyes, they hadn't had a good chance to meet me. Given a minute of quiet, an awful lot of children will spontaneously comment on what happened in the waiting room—the confusion, the nagging, the sibling riot—shedding light on their thinking and family dynamics. My simple interest in these observations goes further than any proclamations I might make in showing my accepting attitude. The words, "You can say anything you want in here," however exuberantly stated, have, in themselves, convinced very few children to spill the beans.

For the first minutes of our hour I allow children to do as they wish. Some children calmly survey the place before taking aim at a particular object or toy. Some go right to my desk and begin drawing, or ask if they may. Some come close; some stay as far away as they can. Nontherapists may be surprised to learn that many sit in the chair opposite mine and begin talking of their troubles, or wait for me to ask about them.

By this time children tend to take notice of the office. Is it a place for children? This, perhaps, is the first question our child patients try to answer for themselves. Children from almost any background and class seem to prefer comfortable, cozy, and unpretentious to its opposite. They prefer offices that look more like living rooms than hospital suites. Children tend to pick cluttered over immaculate, assuming that they will not be expected to be as neat in their play, and maybe even in their thoughts. And as we all know, a good selection of toys, building and drawing materials, and the like can be the quickest route to making children feel welcome (though, to be sure, it takes a lot more than cool stuff to earn their confidence).

As yet knowing pretty much nothing about us, children may look around in an attempt to learn something about the therapist behind the room. Fine furniture and original oil paintings will certainly give a different impression than ripped posters put out by the dairy council or drug companies. Happy childish pictures of sleeping bunnies and dogs dressed in people's clothes may entertain, but give a much different impression than more sedate and ambiguous pictures of roads winding into the woods or a lone bird flying into a muted seascape. Too many diplomas may impress one child, make a second feel inferior, and lead a third to perceptively wonder about the therapist's insecurity. Children begin to read into what they see, but most of the time will keep it to themselves in the first hour, over time testing their hypotheses against the real thing, the therapist.

Of course, many who do child therapy do not have their own offices. They, as students or as practitioners in a crowded clinic, courageously use whatever office is available, however poorly kept or offensively decorated. Other therapists do their work on the road, hauling a bag of toys to children's schools and homes. These therapists know best what the rest of us learn soon enough, that over the long haul it is our psychological presence, not our furnishings or things, that most influences and impresses patients.

To learn and be able to help all we can, we need children and their parents to talk as openly as possible. To talk they must be comfortable. How do we accomplish that?

We might actively seduce them, permitting them to sit on the window sills, offering high tea, or soda and chips, whatever the hour. We might alleviate the slightest hint of tension, theirs or ours, by laughing robustly at things that do not strike us funny or that are unusually perverted. Likewise, we can compliment their parents' choice of clothes or disclose that we, too, have children who wet their beds or disobey us. But these methods carry risk. Children and parents may get the wrong idea of what we do, thinking that we are there to appease them rather than to help them confront their demons and troubles.

By virtue of their being part and parcel of how people act, typical social behaviors have their place in the therapy office. As decades of empty frustration that came at the hands of the old withholding and unreactive analyst have taught us, if we are not human first, we can be nothing to our patients. But they are not the surest means of beginning therapeutic relationships, and can get in the way big time as the therapy proceeds and good times give way to harder ones.

Giving good ear is the earliest and most powerful method we have to engage parents and children. By *good ear* I mean listening that is attentive and caring, listening that truly wants to hear what is being said, not that mostly wants to get another question and another interview out of the way. While patients' words inevitably evoke thoughts and feelings in us, we cannot really listen while planning our next question. While some of us nod, and others "ahem" in understanding, it is the substance of the listening that underlies these signs, the where and how it leads us, that shows parents and children that we are there and interested.

We may have a million questions; we ask a limited number. We ask them slowly. No one likes a third degree, even those who deserve interrogation. Too many questions can shut down the most open and cooperative of us. A handful of open-ended questions answered fully and with ample reflection and interaction will, on the average, inform us more than a lengthy laundry list of items to be asked and responded to machine-gun style.

We go cautiously, reminding ourselves that not every piece of information offered us, however generative of new tangents, is an invitation for further probing. Patients will often tell more than they wish to, and more than they are comfortable with. Learning who our patients are takes time and cannot be jammed into one, two, or even three sessions (even if so mandated by a health care insurer). If there is anything that we as therapists must grow accustomed to, whether conducting an interview or treatment, it is uncertainty and not knowing.

Knowing also means knowing when we don't know. Upon hearing of a dead grandfather, I've made the mistake of inferring sadness and regret, later learning from an embarrassed teenager that, in fact, she was glad "that son of a bitch" had died, a pillar of his community who'd abused his daughter, my patient's mother. I don't assume to know what anything means to another person I'm just meeting. "Why," I'll ask a parent, "do you think Ben (a seventh-grader) is so worried about getting into college now?" Or, "Why, of all the different issues you've raised, are you most upset about Joan's not being more popular?" "What's making you cry?" I'll softly ask a child who weeps. And when she says, "I don't know," I may gently wonder aloud whether she is sure that she really doesn't. Those I ask are often surprised that I question matters or behaviors that tend to be taken at face value. But their varied and unexpected answers confirm the wisdom of my inquiring.

Although we may not like what we are told, our job is neither to judge nor to criticize. We can take for granted that our parents and child patients have already gotten a lifetime's worth of judgment and to little avail. Experiencing our respect for their lifestyle, they—the ones who sought us—frequently will reveal on their own what they think to be amiss or at fault. By *respect* I mean appreciation of the meaning and value that certain life decisions have had for others. I mean neither enthusiastic praise nor tacit endorsement, for it is quite possible that sooner or later I will help parents see why some of their choices have been harmful or deterring to their child—and maybe to themselves. Similarly, we must respect the love that a child has for its parents and families, however abusive or mistreating. To neglect or unilaterally dismiss that love or relationship is to neglect the child.

Our neutrality toward interpersonal conflicts as well as those within the child centers our compass so we can position ourselves to best see all that transpires. I am repulsed, for instance, when a young boy describes torturing animals. But I know that my moral censure will only send this child away to hurt more animals, and perhaps people, including himself. Listening to the gory details and slowly discovering the hurts and injuries that lead to his need for cruel power are the surest key, relatively speaking, to helping him stop his wayward sadism.

Similarly, when I observe a boy and his father wrestle, I do not take sides. My hunches about who is most right almost always prove to be wrong in the long run. Besides, it does (however trite) take two to tango, even when the two are parent and child. Our clear role is to aid both parties in assuming responsibility for their contribution, be it 5 percent or 95.

Fearing criticism and not knowing what to expect, parents and their children may be quite nervous when they come to meet us. Often, just seeing that we are regular people and that our offices have chairs and lamps and wallpaper—not medical machinery or rubber pads—moderates that anxiety. Managing the tension that remains, or which is made anew in response to our interviewing, is another major way to foster comfort.

We don't want patients to feel too stressed to speak and think, or so ill at ease with the process that they abandon therapy before it begins. Nor do we want patients to feel so relaxed that they lose the impetus to do the work that therapy requires. Overly successful attempts to reduce patients' stress can make for easier sessions, but risk letting parents and children leave feeling as alone with their problems as when they came.

How do we concretely manage tension? By going slowly, watching and observing patients' reaction to the interview setting and our comments, for unless we know how to see anxiety, we can do little to handle it. It is easy to see in some children. They visibly shake and sweat, squirm in their seats, put bracelets on and take them off, pick their noses, or experience accelerating tics. Some talk at the speed of light, compulsively interrupt us and themselves, and overflow with a cascade of worry.

Tension can be harder to detect in others. It can hide behind seemingly self-composed personas that are more guarded than confident. Or it can be the motive pushing more aggressive parents to confront us about our credentials or skills before they, so they fear, are attacked first. Likewise, children who seem to want little to do with us may be revealing, not so much an active rejection of us, as a morbid fear of people.

We seldom remark directly on a nervous habit for that makes patients feel criticized and self-conscious and takes away an outlet for tension. But noting the enormity of their anxiety—"You're holding so much worry"—in words that connote the painful burden of being a worrier—can help. Overtly nervous children respond well to calm and steadiness, and occasionally some shared humor concerning their plight. We do not falsely reassure, telling them that they or their loved ones will never die, for that does not reassure and mostly makes us seem like fools.

We go slowly with patients whose anxiety is withdrawn or disguised. When children physically step back, we do not step forward or even lean forward, certain that their retreat is for good and deep reason. We do not force eye contact with children whose eyes are repelled by ours. Or should they be fortressed in their winter coats, we do not rush to invite their taking them off or ask if they want more heat. We assume they feel better with their coats on. When they psychically withdraw, we try to honor that too, letting their neglect of our questions go for now.

As therapists, our flexible use of structure and freedom helps to create a sense of safety. I find that a majority of patients, children and parents, do best with a relatively open-ended atmosphere that, while mindful of the information I need to know, follows their lead.

This is not as true for others. The choice to do or say as they wish can immobilize some anxious and inhibited patients. They prefer some guidance about where to sit, what to talk about, how to play. Rambunctious and impulsive patients are bolstered by greater structure and sharp limits.

Depressive children and parents may have other requisites for comfort and safety. They need therapists who can tolerate great sadness and despair, even this early in the relationship. The glib cheer of a Pollyanna will leave them untouched and awash. They need therapists who take their pain and hopelessness seriously without falling prey to their gloomy outlook. Such patients require enough silence in the hour for their hurts and passivity to surface.

Narcissistic children and parents have especially strong needs not to feel flawed or lacking. Just coming to see a therapist can feel like a frontal assault to the esteem of the narcissistically fragile person. With them we take great care to note the courage—and for parents, the great love, too—implicit in their coming for help. We tiptoe, not out of fear, but to prevent sudden and disruptive deflating of a self-image that, however inflated, is quite shaky. When asked, we answer unusual or abundant questions about our qualifications straightforwardly and nondefensively. We hold these children and parents, like the precious jewels they want to be, with great care lest they drop, break, and flee the shame of therapy.

And then there are the angry parents, and children, who have come with great ambivalence or against their will, under the pressure of a spouse, school, or court. Sometimes simple acknowledgment and acceptance of their reluctant presence defuses their anger, allowing the interview to proceed more smoothly. Others may be comforted and put into a manageable place by our kind but clear stance that we will not be mistreated.

Both parents and children appreciate our sincere interest in their story, in knowing why they have come. "The school says that Joey has ADD." "But what do *you* think?" I ask a parent, my question paying homage to the importance of *their* opinion of *their* child, and suggesting that they will be expected to participate actively. From child to mother to father I go, asking each for his or her version, inviting each to critique or confirm the others' view as seems fit, trying to find and announce the truths and discrepancies that always lie in the middle. "Joey, you're telling me that you can get so wild it scares you. And your parents are telling me that they've been getting on your back, sometimes even being mean, because they don't know what to do when you get that wild. Is that something you all would like help with?" Stated matter-of-factly and in their own terms, parents and child appreciate clear summaries of the reasons they are here.

Our valuing free expression will show itself early and clearly. Unlike the situation with many other authorities in their lives, children are pleasantly surprised, sometimes bemused, to see that they can say whatever they like, however they like. Whether it is sex, aggression, greed, or plain silliness, it's okay in here, they discover. They can put down their teachers, parents, and even me without punishment or retaliation. Our only revenge, they soon see, is to wonder gently what experiences account for their strong feelings and dislikes.

When a young girl stammeringly tries to tell her side of the story to a bullying parent, I hold my finger to my mouth, shushing the parent to let the child get her fair hearing in court. I am no less protective of a devoted mother whose teenage and somewhat abusing son cuts her off at every word. Seeing that my interruptions are not to ridicule or control, but to facilitate their talking, both parents and children start to learn what therapy and I am about.

Although we have an agenda, meaning certain things we want to know, we are bound to it only loosely. We follow the lead of the children and parents—the ones who live their lives first-hand. Their consciouses and unconsciouses know the quickest shortcuts to as well as the most telling detours around the issues and pains underlying their being here. Overactivity—too many questions, too many what-abouts, too many changed subjects—on our part will likely distract us and our patients from the matters at hand and in their hearts.

These generic ways of being with children and their parents in the first meetings give them something immediate and tangible to know about us and therapy, begin to forge a sense of trust and relationship, and promote our gathering the information we need to more formally plan and offer treatment.

2

CAN I HELP YOU?: EVALUATING THE CHILD AND OFFERING TREATMENT

Parents want to feel safe and understood, and want their children to feel the same. But the prime reason they are here is that they want us to stop their child's problem behaviors, relieve her distressing symptoms, and help her cope with difficult life circumstances.

Before we can help, we need to assess the child to determine whether therapy even makes sense, and if so, whether we are the clinicians most suited to provide it. To this end, the early meetings are as evaluative as they are therapeutic.

GETTING TO KNOW THE CHILD

Almost too obvious to mention, the first piece of information we collect is the parents' stated reason for coming. These leading complaints can describe what is most pressing to the parents, or at least what they feel most comfortable sharing at this early stage. "Gwen is failing in school." "Alejandro's been getting stomachaches and not wanting to leave the house." "Billy just seems too angry for a third-grader. Everything throws him into a rage."

For the boy whose parents mention rage, I am particularly watchful for signs of anger or undue frustration. If they are not apparent, I wonder why he doesn't show them to me. Is he overly polite or submissive to me, or does his quickness to flare show itself when he rejoins his parents at the hour's end? Perhaps he is not hot-tempered at all but has a mother who cannot tolerate conflict and who herself is furious much of the time over being abandoned by her husband. Whatever other symptoms and issues eventually show up, however more complex, the parents' original reasons for referral serve to organize our interviewing and formulating.

When we first meet, we are equally interested in hearing what the child thinks are the reasons for his seeing a therapist. Although many children reflexively answer that they don't know, most cannot help but give their side, often interrupting their parents' versions. Even young children can sometimes describe something about why they are here. Of the ones who can't, a good number, with our help, can confirm or negate what we or their parents suggest. Children will frequently cite accurately their bad behaviors and others' disapproval as the main factors for their parents bringing them, filling in the acts and symptoms they themselves are bothered by only if given the time, space, and caring encouragement to do so.

Drawing on our experience with child patients and children we have known in and out of the office, we try to put the parents' and children's perspective into (our) perspective. Are their concerns excessive, like those of one father who saw impending catastrophe in his high school daughter's first C? (His unrealistic standards, not her grade, became the focus of our work.) Or are these concerns out of whack in the other direction? "We know he's been using acid lately, but all the kids are, aren't they?"

The timeliness of the referral provides further understanding. "At least four years," one mother replied to my query as to how long her son had been doing things to hurt himself. "But until this past fall he'd just pull out his hair and scratch himself till he bled."

In several cases I've recalled to myself that the parents seeing me
today had called me one, two, or many years ago and then post-
poned their decision for therapy; some even made appointments
they never kept. Are they frightened, procrastinating, denying parents, I wonder? Or are they ambivalent about getting their child
help or having a clinician meddle in their affairs?

Are the parents interested in the child's perceptions? Most
parents who bring their children are. But some parents, often those
who were pushed here by schools or other agencies, want us to know
only the ways in which their children do bad and disrupt their (the
parents') lives. Such parents grow impatient with us when we ask
their little girl what she thinks and where she hurts. They may read
our interest as weak and pandering to a child they have come to
see as controlling and not to be trusted.

When the main complaint is a specific behavior, we ask concrete questions. When, why, and how much? "Does he mouth off
everywhere or just at home, or maybe just with you?" Whatever
the problem, be it an eating disturbance or school suspension, we
want details. "Tell me," I ask parents and children who fight too
much, "when's the last time you battled? What happened? How
did it start? How did it end? Was it upsetting, uninvolving or . . ."—
yes, families will confirm with embarrassed smiles—". . . fun?" Our
pursuing the facts of a child's life reveals much about their functioning and pulls patients into the gears of therapy.

Knowing what stresses and stressors are ongoing also puts the
referral complaint into a broader perspective. That parents are discussing divorce at home may explain Cindy's sliding grades more
than the bad influence of her new boyfriend, cited by her mother.
Marital tensions, births and deaths, illnesses, financial shifts, moves,
and changes at school are a sampling of the circumstances that can
precipitate new problems and symptoms or motivate the referral
for problems and symptoms that have existed for months.

If the child is suffering, we spend time trying to find out the
precise nature of the angst. When and how much does it hurt? What

makes it worse and what seems to soothe it? When did it begin? Does it ever get unbearable? Do the anxiety and depression seem directly related to a recent incident or dilemma, or are they more entrenched? Does the pain seem to have neurotic meaning, a young girl's body expressing her reluctance to separate? Does it appear to be a sign of more serious illness? Or is this a child, we ask ourselves, who must hurt dramatically to gain the sympathy and nurturing of a self-absorbed mother?

What about the child's general health? This question is especially important for children who come with bodily aches for which doctors can't find a cause. "What happens when you think you're dying?" I've asked a young girl with stomachaches, before turning to ask her mother, "What happens when you think your daughter's dying?" Who are her doctors? How have they managed the child? What has worked and what hasn't? "How does Julie feel about doctors anyway?" I ask. Although I suspect with some certainty that the child's psyche has everything to do with her distress, I explore this area with the same care and thought that guides my queries into the medical life of children coping with chronic and well-documented illness.

I eventually obtain a developmental history, although not in the first session or two. When were milestones achieved? Which ones came precociously and which came late? Have there been separations or other potentially stressing circumstances? How parents negotiate these questions can reveal more than the answers themselves.

We inquire about previous treatment. If other clinicians have been involved we want to know when and for how long, and for what reason they were consulted. "Did it help?" I ask the child. "Did it help?" I ask the parents, following up both with a why or why not. "Did you consider returning to Dr. Black?" I'll ask, perplexed that parents came to me given their and their child's stated esteem for her. Although parents escaping to us from other therapists may flatter us, we can't help but wonder what makes them (and us) think that we'll succeed where, perhaps, other competent clinicians have not.

Cultural and ethnic background are also of great relevance. The meanings of our questions, the meanings of behaviors and symptoms, the meanings of relationships, and the meanings of seeking help and therapy vary among cultures. Some patients are guarded with therapists of a different color or faith. However, assuming that my being green and a worshiper of the star Crypto gives me complete and reliable understanding of every Martian is a mistake. To share a culture or heritage does not guarantee our knowing the private and individual family culture in which a child lives.

However difficult, by the end of the second if not the first hour, I ask virtually all parents whether, to their knowledge, anyone in their child's life abuses drink, drugs, or the child—physically or sexually. If asked without fanfare and apprehension, I've found most parents willing to reply, even when the answers are not happy ones. For the few who are unwilling, their running or less frantic refusal can be the beginning of an answer to what we've asked.

Most of what we learn is told to us spontaneously or in response to what we say and ask. But we can also glean much information by subtler means, such as observing what we see. From the minute our door swings open our search begins. Does the child appear well cared for, well fed, rosy-cheeked, and dressed for the weather? Our worrimeters can't help but go off when we meet a first-grade boy who has black-and-blue bags under his eyes or who wears shorts and a T-shirt on this nippy late autumn morning. Although I may discover soon enough that he is a wayward student, finding a new patient doing his algebra in the waiting room encourages me. Finding that a child has tipped over the magazine table and is now taking apart the thermostat does not.

We watch the children walk and move about the office. Do they trip and bump their way across the room or do they enter gracefully? Do they sit comfortably or do they fidget? I note to myself the blinking tic of one boy and the natural calm of a second. How do they hold and use a crayon? Some children cover the table with an intricate knockdown in the time it takes another to successfully stand just six dominoes. "How does this work?" a slow 10-year-old may ask out of frustration, about to snap a simple twist-to-use pen, whereas the next patient, a first-grader, takes it upon himself to correctly adjust the time on a complicated office clock. And of course, who can miss easy grins, forced smiles, flushed humiliation, and sometimes the saddest faces that lie flat, doing nothing at all. These data, too numerous to imagine or mention, bombard us and allow us to assess varied aspects of the child unobtrusively, such as how coordinated, tense, confident, assertive, able to withstand frustration, energetic, self-protective, and happy he is.

Such observable data can take strange forms. Seeing an adolescent boy pull a handful of dried peas (*where's the slingshot?*), carelessly crumpled paper (*the print looks like something to do with school?*), too much money (*where did he get it, or what's he need it for?*), and a butane lighter (*to smoke, to light fires?*) out of his pocket leads me to question his risk for delinquency, his judgment, and his need to show off to me.

And think of the 4-year-old who carefully blew her stuffed-up nose, managing the entire hour with one tissue. "Excuse me," she said, covering a dainty sneeze with her hand. Compare her with the first-grader who, waving off my offer for even one sheet, wiped his snot over his overalls and my chair when he wasn't coughing fountains of spit over my desk and glasses. We can't draw conclusions from such sparse data, nor can we assume that the more hygienic girl was better adjusted and parented (though she was). But we surely can start to know who these children are.

We generally don't need to ask a lot of odd and distracting questions. Listening to what children say, whatever they say, can show us whether they are oriented in time and space, and whether they can discern outer from inner reality. The sound, style, pace, structure, and vocabulary of their speech, if heeded, can alert us to much about their cognitive functioning and learning experiences, especially that involving language. Clarity and coherence of thought is obvious in an hour's worth of interview, as is the child's ability to listen and understand us. Is the child especially concrete, eccentrically vague and abstract, or does she fluidly go between the two, appropriately for a child that age? Much of a neurological assessment can be done with little effort and ruckus.

We can learn much, too, from watching the child interact with his family. Although a reasonable level of communication, respect, and affection doesn't ensure that all is well at home, I prefer seeing that to a family that marches in coldly, sharing neither a glance nor a word among themselves. In my experience, friendly teasing, particularly genuine smiles and self-disparagement, often goes along with better put together families; biting sarcasm, hostile put-downs, and blaming of others frequently does not.

Who sits where and with whom? Why do my young patient—referred around a learning disability—and her toddler sister cling to their mother's arms, while their father sits passively alone across the room? Do they like her more? Is he somehow toxic or uninvolved with them? Frightened by the interview, do they seek her, not their father, for security? Or, maybe, a narcissistic woman, she demands their rapt attention and audience, ignoring their wish to be near their dad? By taking note now, and as time and events pass, we learn the motives behind what we see. In this case the dynamic proved rather simply, pleasantly, and humbly surprising. The children had missed their mother, who had just that afternoon returned from a three-day trip to care for an elderly aunt. Their father, having spent every hour of the past long weekend with them, was pooped.

Do the parents listen to the young boy? Do they respect his opinion? Do they treat him like a child his age, one much older, a baby or, painfully, like an object? If both parents are present, how do they treat one another? Is the child preferred greatly by one parent and disliked by the other? Does the child seem to be more the wife to her father than does her mother?

How the boy treats his family is no less informative. Does he listen and show respect, or does he cruelly bully his caring, if ineffective, mother? One mildly jealous boy tripped his sister on the way into the office. Another, much more dangerously jealous, devoted his hour to slavishly waiting on his little brother, trying, he later confessed, to deceive me with his overdone show of concern. Every interaction, big or small, carries clues about the child and the social fabric in which she lives and was formed.

Perhaps our most useful source of data is the child's way of being with us. Is eye contact comfortable or hollow, or does the child avoid our gaze as if our own eyes are the halogen headlights of an oncoming truck? Does the child speak with and otherwise treat us like a human being, seeming to have empathy for another and to notice the empathy we have for him? Or might the therapist just as well be a computer or robot that the child can manipulate with a keyboard or remote control? Keeping the child's age and language development in mind, is there give-and-take in our conversation, responsiveness?

Is he trusting and friendly, or does he, as one eighth-grader did, ward me off with a barrage of insults (which, being mostly about my stupidity and queerness, revealed his two biggest fears about himself)? Children, while talking, have occasionally dedicated their hour to neatening my office, handling the stress of the meeting with helpful and conciliatory behavior. Just as commonly, children test me with their uncooperative demeanor, deliberately messing my desk or casually dropping a candy wrapper on the floor with an eye toward my reaction.

What are the child's emotions? Are they assorted and understandable? Are they varied but muted, like a subdued foliage season, or do they come and go with the speed and power of lightning? Does depression or mania prevail? Are his feelings in keeping and proportion with what he is saying? If not, do they betray feelings near the surface, as did one boy's hostility while telling of his pleasure at receiving a much desired birthday gift? Or is the discrepancy between affect and content more worrisome? I've met too many like the sociopathic teenager who couldn't contain his categorical pleasure while describing the skinning of a squirrel he'd killed with a stone. We may meet more seriously ill children whose affect and facial expression are somehow strange, or seem wholly stuck or wholly lacking.

Although the data the child offers is virtually unlimited, I am most interested in the child's honesty with me. When a child admits to remorse, regret, self-hatred, or a wish to change—*and means it*— I am singularly encouraged that therapy will help. A rigid externalizing of responsibility, blaming everyone but herself, worries me.

Assuming we have a good sense of ourselves, how we feel with patients can be a treasure chest of data. A boy talked with glee about the space ride at the county fair, yet I felt an overwhelming sadness. (His mother later told me that he saw his divorced father there with another woman.) And what accounted for my feeling increasingly indifferent to a charming 15-year-old girl's horrid tale of abuse? (I soon found that her intentionally groomed extroversion barely hid a profound vulnerability to dissociate.)

It is my own unexpected or seemingly out-of-line reactions that alert me to something special about what's going on with the child. Needless to say, when using ourselves and our feelings in this way, we must beware of confusing our own unresolved issues and blind spots with those of our patients. The greater experience and self-knowledge we gain by doing therapy, receiving supervision, being in therapy, and continually reflecting on our work generally enhances the reliability of our intuiting.

FORMULATING AND DIAGNOSING

From that virtually limitless sea of clues, we begin to put together the puzzle that is the child. But it isn't the rectangular puzzle we are used to building with our own children. This puzzle has no frame, no flat pieces to set us straight on our path, and it can be almost any shape. Being good at this kind of puzzle requires that we be flexible in our thinking. We need sufficient energy and motivation to try each clue we find, seeing where it fits best, often having to set it aside for now, alongside thousands of other clues, to be sorted through and tried again and again, eventually finding its right place or falling into uselessness.

It is in this intellectually demanding enterprise that theory and facts collide. If we go forth into the consulting room as pure empiricists, persuaded only by what we see, we will be exquisitely open to every possibility. Yet, without any theory or hypotheses about how children work, we may find ourselves immobilized by the volume of information or doing therapy by the seat of our pants, reacting more than deliberating.

Being too convinced of our theories, however, can also retard our work. Believing that we know what has to be can deceive us, leading us to see only the data that supports our theories. Holding onto our theories too rigidly, we are prone to force data into our thinking, rather than using data to inform and guide what we think. It was that kind of intellectual posture that, at its worst, caused well-meaning clinicians to tragically and destructively see "innocent" mothers as agents of their children's autism by having withheld love and nurturing. Clinicians tend to run to their theories when most stressed, confused, or lost . . . precisely the times when more openness and vision are called for. And so we, responsible clinicians, seek a balance, a balance that is fluid, that can both accommodate and assimilate, and that can grow as we learn and experience more of therapy and more of life.

Even with the most well-equilibrated perspective, however, our task is daunting. Though finding a *DSM-IV* diagnosis is easy enough, that does us and our child patients little good.* That freckled red-headed boy who sidled up beside me—affectionately showing me his pet frog, tearful about the polluting of the ponds, missing

---

*A fair discussion of the merits and flaws of *DSM-IV* (1994) is far beyond the scope and space of this book. In short, though such a system has its place—that is, can be justified for reasons of insurance, research, communication, and epidemiology—it barely does any justice to individuals and their treatment.

his divorced father, dreading that I'll bring up his bed-wetting, tortured by his nightmares, struggling with his reading, frustrated by a congenital hip dysfunction, jealous about his younger sister, fearful of his anger, more fearful of being rejected, and worried that his mother has been very tired lately—absolutely and positively, just no way can be neatly stuffed into a jar labeled "307.6 Enuresis," "315.00 Reading Disorder," "300.2 Overanxious Disorder of Childhood," or even the more generous and forgiving "309.0 Adjustment Disorder."

When formulating who a child is, we strive to put the presenting problems into a deservingly complex context that includes all the information we have collected in the first meetings. Only when we begin to know who the child is can we begin to understand the meaning, reasons, and causes of his symptoms and behaviors—and the likely best method to help. Using our good clinical sense, we review our inventory to answer more formally questions concerning the child's intellect, health, reality testing, ego functioning, object relatedness, development of self, conscience, school adjustment, peer relations, family dynamics, and environmental circumstances, both stressing and supporting. Although these psychological terms may intimidate us, as may their demand that we organize our data clinically, by this time we have more than enough information to do what we must.

GIVING PARENTS AND THEIR CHILD FEEDBACK

When, after a number of sessions, we feel that we have seen both child and parents enough to have a good, if beginning, sense of things, we meet with the parents and their child—sometimes together, sometimes apart—to tell them what we think. We include the young girl for the obvious reason that she is the one coming, the one we are talking about. Having come to our meetings and fulfilled her part of the bargain, she is entitled to hear our serious and well-considered assessment of what she's experiencing.

Realizing how vulnerable children and parents are when await-ing the expert's judgment, we generally begin by asking what they are most fearful of hearing. "That she's crazy." "That he's going to be a serial killer." "That he's never going to be happy." Parents' leading questions about how their children are doing often reveal deeper dreads and guilt.

This reminds us of the need to choose our words carefully. While we can't be anything but straight, telling things as they are, we have great latitude in how we share what we've learned, and in the sadder times, how we how we break the bad news. Comparing Johnny's brain to a "broken and poorly wired computer" to com-municate a suspected problem is apt to arouse no less despair than would telling them coldly that their child is abnormal.

Fortunately, there *are* better ways. We use words that people know and understand. Explaining in detail how Johnny wishes to be loved exclusively and that his disruptive antics are intended more to gain affection than to inflict hurt will do more than glibly refer-ring to his Oedipal conflicts. Saying that "when Elaine faces a task that she finds difficult, she tends to avoid humiliation by daydreaming about being a supermodel" does what "Elaine has attention deficit disorder" cannot. Doesn't describing how a child doesn't do some-thing so well in certain situations beat a vague reference to his dys-function?

We respect the value of clarity, which nearly every worthy book on the craft of writing extols. When an author writes obscurely, worships big words, overuses the passive voice, and gets lost in endless sentences that say little, there's a good chance that he's not sure what he wants to say. Out of insecurity, and fear, some clini-cians state their findings so tentatively and with so much qualifying that it's hard to know what has been said.

We tell parents and their child almost anything we feel is of value, and we try particularly to explain the possible meanings of the referring complaint and the strengths and weaknesses that the child and family bring to that issue. When we must share our sense that something is seriously amiss, we don't rush to get it over, blurting out "mental illness." We go slowly, our care itself warning parents that something is coming and giving them time to begin processing what we'll be telling them. We do not speak first of *psychosis*, but instead describe the difficulty their child has distinguishing outer reality from what he imagines, elaborating how this varies under different stresses as well as ways in which it has been adaptive and protective. Our efforts are not to avoid something bad; they are meant to avoid shocking a parent with one awful word so they become unable to hear and understand anything further. After a lengthy discussion of what a lack-of-reality testing means for their child, for example, it is not unusual for a parent to then ask if that is what *psychotic* means, a question we then answer directly in the affirmative.

When parents take the blame unfairly for their child's problems—such as autism or a learning disability—we try to offset their self-criticism. But in cases where parenting and home life have been detrimental, we do not lobby for their self-forgiveness and rush to relieve their guilt. Nor do we make light of their having delayed treatment for years.

After sharing our sense of what is going on, we address what therapy can do. Here again our work is challenging. Father may want a better behaved Tony. Mother may want a happier Tony. School may want a harder-working Tony. Tony wants a more confident Tony and one that his parents will like more. Everyone's vision of goals is relevant here, and usually they are compatible.

Short-term goals versus long-term. Big goals versus little. Inner goals versus outer. Do we want symptom relief, changed behavior, more insight, better self-control, increased resilience, more connectedness, or just a more cooperative daughter?

When offering treatment, we do not promise the world—sometimes because we don't think it will be forthcoming, more often because only time and therapy will tell. But neither do we prematurely predict what may never happen. I have worked with too many children whose parents were told—wrongly, time proved—that their child would never ride a bicycle or drive a car (he is a skilled cyclist and driver), never succeed in even the lowliest classroom (as she came out of her cocoon she showed herself to be gifted and is now a college student), never throw a ball (became a varsity athlete), never relate to friends like other children (became a class officer), and never work at anything (now an earnest and self-motivated lobbyist for the environment). Gloomy predictions seldom add anything, especially at this very early stage.

We do not push parents, or children, to make a decision on the spot, though a majority of them do. We watch carefully for signs of ambivalence or confusion, meeting them head-on. We know that sweeping such tensions under the rug will not get rid of them, and may lead to much bigger resistances later on. "Of course you are unsure about this whole idea," I easily said to one skeptical father. "Bringing your child to a therapist is a strange business." Accepted in his uncertainty, this father was then able to reveal his having had a bad experience with a therapist years ago as well as his current fear that I might do badly by his son.

When parents agree to bring their child to us for therapy, they have entrusted us with their most cherished possession. At the very least, all of our assessing and interacting with the child and parents up to this point should attest to our recognizing the privilege and responsibility of that decision.

3

THE NOT-SO-MAGIC
OF THERAPY:
HOW THERAPY WORKS

Psychotherapy can appear to be a rather strange and mysterious business. Some see us as doing our good, or bad, by some form of psychic voodoo, exerting a magical influence upon another's mind. Many, even some clinicians, judge that, for all of our fancy theory and prices, we help mostly by being a good friend to someone who's hurting or confused. What, in fact, does therapy do, and how does it do it?

MAKING A SAFE PLACE

The issue of safety is one that underlies so many aspects of what happens in treatment. Why would anyone, no less a child, want to spend time with, or maybe even open up or grow close to, someone who posed a danger?

> In his first four sessions 14-year-old Kevin wore an oversized turtleneck stretched over his lower face. Through this cotton veil, his

muffled voice spoke about his "stupid, ugly teachers," the "stupid, ugly girls" in his class, and his "stupid, ugly parents." He even put down the "stupid, ugly" dog he saw outside my office (a neighbor's bright and handsome, if jumpy, golden retriever), seeming to have no awareness of just how frequently he used those precise and demeaning words. Knowing from his mother that Kevin believed his chin was somehow misshapen, his self-consciousness making daily life an unbearable ordeal, I did not push his face into what he said or what he wore, but instead patiently waited.

In his fifth hour Kevin asked me if I knew why he hid his face. Neither surprised nor bothered by my affirming nod, he expressed gratitude that I'd let him be the one to bring up the subject. "You know," he added, pulling his turtleneck down for the first time, "I just tripped over the dog, and she's really not ugly at all."

My respect for his guardedness made Kevin feel safe enough to bring up the real reason he was here, a chin that, while hardly monstrous, had become a repository for his seeing himself as the stupid and ugly one. My waiting allowed Kevin, in his own time, to take ownership of his reason for coming and to voluntarily join forces with me and the therapy. Without such therapeutic allying— a process that grows and grows throughout a sound course of therapy—we therapists are essentially controlling masters who push and pull our stubborn donkeys along the trail.

To do therapy requires that a child look at herself. Our looking at her, though helpful, is not enough. But to look at herself she must expose her most precious goods—what she thinks, feels, does, says, plays, and draws—putting her at risk of the therapist's ridicule, rejection, or otherwise negative reaction. Although we might stand on our desks and loudly proclaim that we would never ever do such things, it is only our unwavering acceptance—in good and bad, and over time—that will convince her she is in trustworthy company.

For the traumatized child the safety of therapy provides an immediate shelter, a place where she can't be hurt or abused for the moment and, perhaps, ever again. She needs first to be rescued from harm's way. Only when safe from abuse and neglect can she, and we, afford to look at the damage and begin restoring what we can. Only when she knows she is no longer in danger can she start to make sense of her experience. Her soiled trust, like that of any abused child, must be earned back. As long as we live in a house made of straw or mud, we should be wary of the wolf. Unfortunately for children whose love and trust have been betrayed, or who have suffered more random violence or tragedy, even walls of brick and steel do not make for feelings of security. The haven of therapy serves increasingly as a fortress in which the child can work on better understanding and growing past her trauma.

The safety of therapy can let a mildly hampered child catch his breath. The nonjudgmental atmosphere of therapy gradually invites children to let down not just their hair, but their swords and shields, too. "Geez, what a relief," said one big bully some weeks after having shared that he's petrified of insects. To have found a place where he could start to be himself both felt and did good in itself.

Throughout treatment, but especially early on for those who for too long have held onto stress or pain, the safety of therapy allows for catharsis and abreaction, the letting go of feelings. For weeks some children will hold onto their tears while remembering Muffin or their favorite grandfather, their faces crunched, their eyes swollen red, their brows quivering, feeling that boys shouldn't cry or that, once begun, they'll never be able to stop. But when they do, they usually feel better. Although sobbing and wailing in themselves do not make for a treatment, and generally do not lead to growth, they can relieve a great deal of pressure and sometimes bring unexpected insights.

Laura's parents had brought the 13-year-old because she was sleeping poorly, eating little, and not seeming her cheery self. A few weeks into therapy it was already clear that Laura—good student, daughter, and friend—was the salt of the earth. Why, she would even take her retarded younger sister with her to the mall. "If they don't have room in their hearts for her, then I don't have room in mine for them," Laura told me.

Not knowing where this might lead, I didn't praise the goodness that was so evident. This proved to be sound when Laura, months later—talking about receiving a helping award from the Special Olympics—suddenly began crying. "What is it, Laura?" I asked.

"I'm a rotten person," she wailed. "I'm not at all the good girl people think I am. It's me that should have been born retarded. It's me that should be dead."

What Laura meant, we came to see, went further than her survivor guilt, her having intellectual gifts that her sister did not. The thought that she "deserved to die," that she be sentenced to death, came from an even darker place. "Sometimes I wish she were dead," Laura finally gasped between sobs. "I don't want to spend my whole life taking care of her," she explained. "I don't want to spend my whole life feeling bad 'cause I'm not retarded, too." As long as Laura had held back her tears, she was able to hold back the pained sentiment behind them.

The refuge of therapy, including the therapist's steady presence, can allow a child to grieve a recent loss. That loss need not be a death, but can be the unavailability of or profound disappointment in a person, or the loss of a child's ideals of what she or life should be. Often, and with more difficulty, that same refuge can permit a delayed or stunted bereaving to reawaken, surface, and pass. Not uncommonly, children who save their mourning are children who temperamentally tend to hold in their feelings or who come from homes where such sadness cannot be tolerated.

The dependable quiet and calm of therapy is particularly critical to the work for children who are easily overstimulated. An overly cluttered office and, even worse, an overly cluttered therapist run the risk of maintaining the distractible child in overdrive, obstructing his use of treatment. For the thin-skinned child the emotional insulation of therapy—meaning mostly that the therapist expects nothing much from the patient and keeps his own feelings to himself—is itself reparative. Like turtles midst a flock of seagulls, such children, sensing danger everywhere, remain in their shells, lest they be forced into contact with people and their feelings. Only by allowing them to keep their shells on for protection and security might they someday be willing to stick their necks and heads out.

Providing this insulating function can be tough work for the therapist. Work with high-functioning autistic, or Asperger's, children shows how difficult it is to give a child all the aloneness he needs. To truly feel what this child feels about us means feeling unneeded, unwanted, noxious, dangerous, and as having needs and feelings that the child deeply does not want to be around. Yet, if we push ourselves over their doorsteps, we can lose them for a long time, if not forever.

In addition to respite from their abuses, the safety of the therapy office offers traumatized children repeated opportunity to begin mastering their tragic, and sometimes dehumanizing, experiences. But again, our supplying that stable setting isn't always easy.

> Russell, a sixth-grade boy whose utter lack of self-confidence clashed with his good brains, looks, and musical talents, was oblivious to me. He intently pushed the end of one paper clip into the other, over and over again, in and out, until, remembering I was there, with embarrassment he threw the clips into the wastebasket. Some weeks later he brought his own jumbo clip to sadistically jam, with all his might, through the middle of a normal-sized paper clip. Slower than slowly, Russell elaborated this activity—jabbing pencils, soda bottles, and then his fingers into big globs of clay, until, one day, shocked by his having stuck a pencil into my couch, he confessed having been molested by a male babysitter as a young child.

I knew he'd been abused before we'd ever met; his parents had told me. He and I had even discussed it during the first meetings. But he'd forgotten . . . he had to. I knew enough to know that Russell's belabored preoccupation with paper clips and stabbing carried significance and needed to be given room for its expression. Fortunately, I was secure enough to tolerate the feelings that expression, and all that it implied, evoked. Had I been too repulsed, frightened, or in some other way uncomfortable with what I'd learned, I likely could not have preserved the therapeutic space so well, likely distracting both of us with observations about his aggression or unrelated issues or asking questions about, perhaps, his schoolwork.

The safe space we create also allows for the playing out of developmental tasks in the service of their mastery.

> "Well, I'm going now. I'm leaving home," 5-year-old Ginger said sweetly for the moose puppet.
>
> "Goodbye," I said, watching Ginger's arm hide the moose behind her back. But he wasn't gone for long.
>
> "Surprise!" Ginger exclaimed, the moose suddenly back in my face.
>
> How nice to see you again!"
>
> "Gee, it's great to be back," Ginger's moose replied. "But I think I have to leave again. Bye." And so it went, on each trip moose going farther away and for a longer time.

Five-year-old Ginger wanted to go to kindergarten but she didn't like leaving her home. Her mom, having lost her own mother when in early elementary school, had comparable doubts about Ginger's going off. But Ginger's play suggested that her wish to go was greater than her fear. A rather healthy child from a good home, who sensed the safety of my office and me, Ginger spontaneously went to work in her first session. In a handful of hours Ginger's reenacting of a moose–child's leave-taking and rapprochement cleared the way for an open discussion of her worry that being a big girl at school might cost her some dependency and nurturing. She soon was off and running.

In a related fashion, children who've felt small, helpless, and otherwise powerless in the face of big and little insults use the permissive and secure aspect of therapy to revise history. In her play a real–life victim can cast herself as a hero. A good girl, who outside therapy lacked any appreciation for her less–than–holy thoughts, plays an evil witch. Perpetually beat up and made fun of by his older brother, a boy comes in weekly to be the tyrant. More than a few children play school, notoriously assuming the role as the bossy teacher. By being the one in control, children come to better understand and cope with the many life situations in which they must bend to authority and rules.

The ways by which the sanctuary we create enables and furthers a course of therapy are as numerous as they are indispensable. No one has taught us these core principles better than the client-centered school of child therapy. For example, read the instructive, lively, and rich work of Virginia Axline, Haim Ginott, and Clark Moustakas. However, contrary to their view, I do not think that a nonthreatening, nonjudging, and nondirecting atmosphere, while imperative, is enough for most children's therapies. Children will indeed unfold and blossom when given the psychic equivalents of sunlight, water, and rich soil, but only to a point. Most of us, children included, have blind spots, conflicts, trauma, and other vulnerabilities that we hide and protect even in what appear to be the most open and welcoming of settings. Even in the arms of the kindest of therapists, children need to be confronted, informed, or otherwise acted upon to find relief and move ahead.

HOLDING

Perhaps the most basic, powerful, and yet difficult function we serve is to hold our patients.

> "I'm going to eat my shit out of myself and then stuff it in my mother's breasts and shoot her and me on an alien ship to Pluto and then come back and then and then I'm and then I'm going to stuff my head in

a dog's ass and walk to school, barking at everybody, and peeing on their shoes, and when my spaceship gets back from Pluto me and my mom will have a baby that drinks acid and likes to eat toxic waste and it'll grow real big and it'll do sex with everybody and . . ."

Drew's soliloquy moved nonstop and at the speed of light. Each metaphor grew more divergent and disturbing than the last. If I had bailed out on him, simply admitting that what he spoke of, and his deteriorating state, was too much for me, no one would have faulted me. Previous clinicians had judged him to be too ill to be helped by outpatient therapy.

They were wrong. With just weekly meetings he'd managed in regular schools for the previous two years, and had become dramatically less hostile, aggressive, and susceptible to stress. In my view, this more recent regression was a positive sign that he was bringing his more crazed self into the treatment, something he'd previously shown more when stressed outside of the therapy office.

". . . And then and then the baby is going to grow a big dick and shove it everywhere and bite his crib and eat his crib and his Popeye mobile and then he's going to fly into the sky and fly back to earth . . ."

Drew neither halted his story nor did he behaviorally break down. I could see that he was not truly out of control, but was sharing something important, however intense and undifferentiated.

"And then he's going to poop and poop and poop more poop than everyone's ever seen, all over his school. No one's going to be able to find the school it'll be so lost in that mountain of crap."

By the end of the session Drew had quieted as had his story. Unafraid of his words, and of the primitive impulses and thinking behind them, I did little but listen to keep with him. I didn't interrupt him, nor did I distract him. I didn't stop to question him about sexual abuse, or suicidal ideation, or his relationship with his mother. Knowing that he was functioning at home and school, if with some struggling, I didn't take his psychotic-sounding ranting as a sign that he needed inpatient treatment (whatever that is, these days).

> "School. A school covered in poop," I said aloud, aware that the final and more coherent words probably carried the message, if there was one. "Is something going on in school?"

There was, Drew told me. Lots. A failed spelling exam. Being embarrassed by a teacher's flippant remark. Tripping to the floor in gym. But more than everything Drew was panicked over a school project for which he was giving a small talk the next day—a talk which, to his and my surprise, went uneventfully well.

By emotionally containing Drew—"You don't get freaked out by my crazy stuff like everyone else does"—I allowed him to feel and express without having to bear the burden of hurting, terrifying, or repelling me, and without the fear of being punished or hospitalized for exposing himself. My steady presence in the wake of his explosion somewhat detoxified the awful things that tormented his insides. By sharing the horrendous ways in which he feared losing self-control, ways that held sane and understandable meaning, he actually came to have more control over himself.

Although we don't cradle our patients physically, we hold our patients like mothers do their babies. When our patients are colicky or overstimulated with anger or irritation, we stay right with them, calming them with *our* calm, using ourselves, like sponges, to absorb and regulate some of the affect that torments them. That the most petite of woman therapists can comfort and contain the brawniest of male patients demonstrates the psychological power of our holding. Although that wild and enormous teenager may know that I could never single-handedly restrain him—bigger adults in his life have tried—he somehow feels safe with me, meaning safe from himself, his thoughts, and what he might do.

We can hold our patients in relation to almost any feeling or worry, lending them ego that they—at least for the moment—are lacking. For example, ninth-grader Bobby came to a session angry enough to kill another child who'd ridiculed him in front of a prospective girlfriend. By sharing his rage with me, however (who neither pushed it away nor tried to talk him out of it), he came to his own senses, saw more clearly why he was so incensed, and came up with a solution that wouldn't hurt either himself or his rival. For children who lack personal definition, or are prone to fragment under stress, our holding can be a primary means of helping restore or integrate their various parts into a whole.

Our holding, although concentrated at certain points (such as during a panic or in a phase where suicidal thinking is prominent), occupies most every moment of every sound therapy, helping our patients tolerate and face the therapeutic work and discomfort without having to flee, disintegrate, or attack. While especially important for child patients whose parents are unwilling or unable to hold them (because of their own deficits or as a result of a mismatch with their child's temperament), it matters even to the child from a high-functioning and nurturant home. In the best of treatments this holding—an inner sense that we and therapy are with them—endures beyond the office walls, helping our patients to function, cope, stay out of trouble, and suffer less for the six days and twenty-three or so hours when they are not with us.

INTERVENING

Just as our holding psychologically replicates an aspect of the mother and child relationship, some of our other therapeutic functions also both borrow from and seek to promote natural and good human development. Mothers mirror what their young children think and feel, and we try to do the same with our patients. "You really are sad today" or "You don't want me telling your parents" confirms our patients' experiences, helping to solidify their own convictions. Our getting it right and making it clear—meaning genuinely, not by rote or empty parroting—is most valuable to the child who has been raised to rely not on her own thoughts and feelings, but on those of a narcissistically fragile parent. But this applies to all children in therapy, for they all have aspects of themselves that are more false than others, areas in which they are less trusting of their own perceptions and sentiments.

Parents also tend to admire and take pleasure in their children's growth, such as the first steps or adorable, if awkward, beginnings of speech. As therapists we too encourage our patients by noting their courage in doing therapy and taking pride in their efforts. "How brave of you, Molly," I said to a girl who, rather than start a fight with her classmates, shared the underlying frustration with her teacher. Therapy often intercedes in areas where decent parents have been unable to celebrate their child's developing, for example, a loving mother who, herself fearful of separation, rejects her child whenever he takes a healthy giant step toward independence, or a compulsively clean father who rejects his dear son's adventurousness because of the dirt and bugs that come along. The authentic satisfaction that we as therapists derive from every inch of our patients' progress and efforts, however messy or autonomous, helps revive their developmental momentum in those blocked areas.

Empathy, a hallmark of the good child–parent relationship, is also crucial to effective psychotherapy. More than walking in another's shoes or taking his perspective, empathy means understanding, and conveying that you understand, another's feelings or situation. Sometimes we demonstrate our empathy in our heartfelt reflecting, "It's just so discouraging." Sometimes we empathize by doing things, such as handing a box of tissues to a child whose eyes are welling, our gesture saying, "It's okay, you can cry." At other times, realizing that our words aren't wanted or won't be helpful, we empathize by means of our silent presence or by nodding goodbye instead of exuberantly wishing a good week. Any manner of intervening that is intimately sensitive to where the child is emotionally and to what she needs is empathic.

The feeling of empathy, of being understood, is one we all enjoy and want, and one that in itself heals, especially the child whose home is lacking in it. In times of misbehavior, letting him know that *his* plight is understood ("You feel picked on by everybody") can help a defensive child let his other-blaming guard down and look at what he might have done.

Our steady empathy throughout therapy serves not only to bathe the child in understanding but also to set the stage for the many and inevitable moments when we misunderstand the child. These lapses, so-called empathic failures, offer some of the most therapeutically powerful opportunities in a course of treatment.

> "I said something wrong, didn't I?" I spoke just loud enough to be heard. But no response came from under the chair where Brian had curled himself up. His trombone lay on the floor where'd he'd dropped it and himself one instant after I'd praised his playing. He'd come to therapy directly from school band rehearsal. A perfectionistic and brittley shy child, even his agreeing to do band was a major victory, as striking as his suggesting that he play a concert for me.
>
> The session passed, Brian in his cave, until in the final minutes he spoke. "I play awful and you know it. Why'd you say I played nicely? That's like making fun of me."

My words that he'd played nicely, however well intentioned, did anything but make Brian feel good. If we'd stopped here, Brian would have left feeling worse and smaller than when he came, cursing the moment he'd decided to bring his instrument along. But we didn't.

With my urging Brian acknowledged comparing his playing to that of his accomplished teacher, not to standards more fitting a novice trombonist. Brian assumed that I was as disappointed in his playing as he was. His coming to see how my injuring his pride and his image of himself led to his withdrawing brought a long inch of growth to his becoming less self-criticizing and likely to give up activities that he enjoys. Over the course of Brian's therapy, with its many empathic failures and their repair, the accumulation of many such inches, then feet, brought him increased and lasting resiliency in the face of the slings and arrows that pervade daily life.

It is our empathy that enables us to gauge where children are in terms of tension and affect so that we intervene at the proper time and to the right degree. We seek to push them to deal with as much as they can adaptively. To overwhelm their resources will be destructive and set them back; to underwhelm them will support the status quo, inviting regression and complacency. By titrating how much we emotionally confront children—ever striving to provide the optimal amount of intervention—we psychically exercise them. This slow and steady work exercises children's capacities to tolerate and manage their emotions, making them less irritable and less impulsive.

Ultimately, much of therapy is motivated by the hope of change. But people must change themselves, even rather young and small people. To change, a child first has to notice that a problem exists, see what is. For this reason, helping children to see themselves and their predicaments honestly is one of our prime functions as therapists. We do this in a number of ways.

"I put out the fire and pulled the alarm. If it weren't for me, everything would have burned down. They should give me a medal or reward," 13-year-old Evan declared. "They really should."

Evan spoke of his bravery loudly, but his quieter twitching and reluctance to look at me told me otherwise. Only after some forty-eight minutes of crowing, and my simply listening, did he admit to having accidentally lit a brush fire. By not putting him on the defensive immediately, as I easily could have, his conscience led him to confess his crime. Once he could describe and see his situation for what it had been, he was able to therapeutically explore his occasional recklessness, his poor judgment when so stressed, and his difficulty owning up to his misdeeds.

Much of our intervening is simply to help children face the mirror with the lights on and their eyes open. "What makes it so hard to tell me what happened?" I may ask a child, knowing that the reasons likely carry more significance than do the facts of what actually transpired. "You always say good, fine, no problem when I ask about school," I note to another, my noncritical words suggesting that perhaps any other answer is intolerable. To a third, "You say you hate being so mean, but you spent every minute of the hour trying to humiliate your sister in front of me." By gently confronting I try to encourage my child patients to see it like it is and to see themselves as they are.

By maintaining a neutral stance not toward the young girl, but toward her conflicts, we enable her to examine all angles fully. For example, if she speaks of her need to do the right thing, I may wonder about her temptation to do the wrong. In one case I asked myself why she is protesting so vigorously about the dangers of taking acid. I learned that her noisy statement about prohibition betrayed her concealed, if conflicted, plan to try acid at a concert that weekend, a plan she decided to abandon following our discussion. A more pointed assault on my part would have sent her hidden agenda and ideas about drugs even farther underground.

Much of our work intends to bring about insight. Although psychoanalytic schools propose varied and complex definitions, I agree with Webster's (Merriam-Webster 1993): insight is "the power or act of seeing into a situation" [or oneself—*me*].

"I'm evil. Pure evil." Adam spent the first of his hours working hard to convince me of his utterly rotten character, berating me and everyone else with foul and demeaning language. "I don't care about nobody and nothing," he said more than once.

But this teenager gave himself away in the twelfth hour. Cruelly celebrating having seen a dead dog up the street, he suddenly interrupted himself to ask whether it might have been my dog. My noting his obvious concern led to a crashing down of his gangster persona, and his coming to note that, not only did he care, but that his caring made him feel exquisitely vulnerable to harm and disappointment. He came to see that he was much more a good boy than a bad one.

We ofttimes raise insight by bringing what is unconscious to awareness. Coming to recognize that she had deeply buried fantasies of marrying her father and that she felt guilty about so wanting to outcompete her beloved mother, a young adolescent tomboy transformed into a feminine and confident young woman who could identify with both parents. Conversely, recognizing his occasional wish to be a girl allowed a heterosexual high school student to pursue drama studies, a creative interest he'd abandoned out of homophobia.

In these instances specific fantasy wielded obstructive powers. At other times we help our child patients to remember what has been repressed.

> Curtiss, a bright boy, was having serious troubles in junior high school. He felt constantly preoccupied, though he didn't know why. "I don't know what it is," he explained, sincerely perplexed. His self-consciousness led to many absences, particularly to avoid any school activity that involved any sort of exposure. He was unable to speak in class, let alone give an oral report. And being near girls was the worst. He worried that he might commit a sex crime or pee in his pants.

Curtiss' cure came quickly enough. Having gone with his mother to pick up his little cousin from preschool, he found himself about to pass out while passing the classroom's bathroom door. In therapy that sensation led to his spontaneously recalling having wet himself in kindergarten while waiting for his teacher to get out of the bathroom. Of course, a majority of unrepressed traumata do much more damage and require much more therapeutic working through than the recalling of them, however eventful that in itself can be.

Likewise, insight can be had by reuniting distress with its proper source. Children unable to tolerate the pain of losses and tragedies—or even much smaller narcissistic injuries—are prone to deposit their distress into undeserving, confusing, and obstructing places. I've frequently seen children whose sudden deterioration in school, we eventually learned, was caused by unexpressed fears that their parents would divorce. Once they put their fears out in the open, these children could take action. Some questioned their parents and learned that their fears were unfounded. Others, who discovered that divorce was imminent, could at least take action to better understand and cope with the sad reality that was coming.

Insight also comes when children can understand how they manage their life and its stresses. "I withdraw from classmates not, as I've believed, because they're beneath me, but because I fear my loving them and their leaving me." "I endlessly and compulsively line up my things not because I value neatness, but because it soothes my ever-present sense of doom." "I brag not because I am so great, but actually because most of the time I feel quite small and insignificant." "My promiscuous interest in sex does not attest to my maturity and appeal as much as it reflects my need for attention and something to help glue together my fragmented self."

Few children, of course, will ever speak these precise words. But over time, and with our support and respect for the important adaptive and protective functions these self-deceits have served, our patients often speak words that mean the same, their accompanying insights leading to more genuine ways of being and more openness to the therapeutic process.

In particularly intense therapies that run longer, transferential reactions, in which the child experiences the therapist as somehow being like a significant person from life outside of therapy, can facilitate insight.

My work with Johnnie had gone splendidly. He ran to the office, seeing me as someone he could admire and as someone to admire him back. Within two months much of his disruptive behavior had vanished. However, his migraines had grown more frequent and severe. This discouraging phase was accompanied by a dramatic shift in our relationship. Johnnie began to see me as unreliable and judgmental. He called me a bum and a loser. He began to experience me as colossally critical of him. He heard my softest sigh as a sign of boredom, my benign questions as frontal attacks, and our meeting only once weekly as indisputable proof that I wished to see him as little as possible and that I hated him.

Over many sessions, his certainty that I disliked him grew to the point where he tried to avoid his sessions, pleading with his mother not to make him come into my office. "Do you know what it's like to be with someone who hates you?" he screamed inches from my face. "Do you? Do you?" My comment that I was certain he did, brought a flood of tears and the acknowledgment that his alcoholic, abusive, and now dead father had never had a kind word or smile for Johnnie.

Too pained to remember his father more consciously, Johnnie began to fill in my portrait with colors and shades of a man he knew much better than me. I became as awful as his father, with the difference, however, that he could confront me and we would work it out, just as we did. His rage expressed, in effigy, to the man who deserved it, Johnnie's migraines subsided, eventually vanishing completely as he became better at managing his own considerable temper. He also became more comfortable having good, more complex relationships with male adults and peers, no longer needing to see them as either all good or all bad.

One doesn't have to have a full-blown transference reaction to use the therapist in that way. Quite commonly, children (and their parents) come to therapy suffering from harsh consciences that seldom if ever give them a break. Their self-criticism is easily projected onto the relatively undefined therapist. "You don't like me."

"You don't want me to get a lot of presents." "You agree with my mother and think I was wrong." "You're just like my principal." We can help such children grow to live more freely and have more compassion for themselves by demonstrating patiently, and over much time, that they are the ones condemning themselves.

For all of our fancy terminology and deep theories, we as therapists help in other, simpler ways, too. We educate, showing our child patients how the world can work, how people work, and how they can have greater influence in that world. With our respect, honesty, and earnestness, we set an example, showing children how we conduct ourselves, sometimes inspiring them to emulate us. We help them learn to be better problem solvers, clarifying their options and empowering them to make more effective choices in their own best interests. At times we employ behavioral methods too, encouraging their parents to build more structure into home life, for example, or to gently but steadily expose their children to the situations that frighten them.

In the end, therapy helps mostly by helping children cope and live with their limitations and circumstances, enabling them to grow as fully and richly as possible. For some children these limitations mean severe disabilities, these circumstances mean horrid abuse. For others it is no more and no less than the basic challenge of growing up and human existence that pains them. Whatever our approaches or methods, our goal is to heal what's been hurt, repair what can be fixed, and allow natural development to proceed. However sophisticated or impeccable our clinical work, it is largely our enduring interest, affection, and respect for the child's humanity and selfhood that carries much of our therapeutic powers. Though love is hardly enough, and the notion of the corrective emotional experience goes only so far, I am convinced that it is children's learning to truly, not narcissistically, love themselves that makes for the most progress, a transformation that can occur only with therapists who really do like them.

4

DO FENCE
ME IN:
THE BOUNDS
AND LIMITS

Much of what takes place in psychotherapy occurs in the ether of human relationships, beyond our overt words and actions, in the recesses of our patients' and our own psyches, and everywhere between. It involves an ever-flowing interchange between two people in a more or less open atmosphere that can appear rather chaotic and defying of logic. But certain structures and reasons guide and ensure this sometimes glaring, sometimes subtle process.

THE FRAMEWORK

Consider a professional soccer game in which no rules apply, players run in and out as they please, picking the ball up with their hands, passing it around like a basketball, kicking and tackling one another, ignoring the time-out whistles; lesser players deliberately hurting superior ones or wildly climbing into the bleachers to beat on jeering spectators while equally outraged fans rush onto the field to assault the opposing team. Such anarchy might make for a cheap moment of excitement, but it would soon destroy the sport. Fans would avoid the stadium out of fear, as might star players. And as the level of play plummeted, television and newspaper interest in the sport would dry up.

Although the structure that oversees soccer can seem stifling, the fact that there are discrete stands for the fans, a well-demarcated field, and official rules for the players and referees to keep it all in check is ironically what permits the action to be so robust, spontaneous, unpredictable, and genuine. Similarly, it is the sound and sturdy framework of therapy—framework being the dependable conditions and terms under which we meet the patient—that guarantees safety and allows for the therapeutic process to evolve so freely, passionately, and productively.

The Space

Space is the first dimension of therapeutic reality. Its being well-defined and enduring are what carry the most weight in a therapy.

> "Boingy, boingy, boingy. . . ." Circling the office, Raymond threw his body against every inch of wall. "Yup, they're okay." He opened and shut the windows. "In case a fire starts, but we probably have to worry more about burglars," he explained, tapping hard on the glass with his knuckles. "Strong enough." He did several heavy jumping jacks to see that the floor could hold us. Then, without a smile, he tried to slide his feet under the door as if to prove that he wouldn't fit. "If I want to leave, I guess I'll just have to open the door. And no one can sneak in either, unless they're a snake. Iiiiiii'm not crazy," he then screamed at a tonsil-shaking volume until satisfied that the walls, windows, and overhead light hadn't cracked. "We're set for now," he announced, sounding rather unconvinced.

Raymond was a dangerously reckless and destructive child. Seeing the office as a six-sided box akin to a wild animal's cage—

this perception grounded in his burgeoning delinquency as well as more fantastic fears of being imprisoned in a dungeon—he had to check the walls, floor, and ceiling. Aware that he couldn't rely on his own skin and ego to keep his thoughts and impulses contained, Raymond asked the right questions of therapy through his behavior. Can this office keep me safe from the outside world? Can this office keep the outside world safe from me? These concerns took a shortcut to his even deeper concern: Can this office—and the therapist within—keep me safe from myself? The sturdy walls of therapy served Raymond and his therapy from hello to good-bye, enabling him to bring his more troubled self into the work, and leading to a strengthened ego and greater self-control.

Although my office is far from perfectly soundproofed, children learn quickly that what they say can't be heard by the parents and siblings who wait for them. Nor can what they do be seen. More symbolically, they appreciate that what they say in here can't be heard by friends, family, teachers, who are nowhere near my office. This physical insulation permits children to open up more freely to me, themselves, and the therapy without fear of hurting loved ones' feelings or being retaliatively punished for having spoken negatively of them.

For the less impulse-ridden child, the walls of therapy define a space that becomes his own, even if only once a week. This enclosure makes clear that unless one of us flees, we—therapist and child—are stuck with each other for fifty minutes. While this can be burdensome for the youngster who truly hates therapy or is navigating through a tough therapeutic phase, children routinely come to cherish this physical assurance of my being with them. After all, how often does a child get to lock himself and a beloved parent in a room together, not to be disturbed for an hour?

The physical substance of the office contributes to the holding function of therapy. Children lean against the wall or slide to the floor in more regressed moments. In these highly vulnerable times they can rest easy, knowing they will not be assaulted, stoned, or pummeled by a younger brother. Only when children sense a secure place can they expose their psychological underbelly.

That we meet with a child in a single room that is cut off from all other rooms and the world conveys an important message: as long as we have you and me in the office, we have everything we need to do therapy—the implied corollary is that as long as we have you and me in here, we have everything we need to make a relationship. In order to do our work, we need no more than our mutual judgments and interactions. In this context it only makes sense that children who are particularly uncomfortable with feelings and people can initially find the therapy office confining and unnerving.

Repeatedly experiencing this discrete and discreet space physically gives children a concrete home for their emotions and selves. Just as they affiliate skating with the rink, learning with school, and running wild with the playground, they come to associate being themselves with the therapy office. Assuming a good-enough therapy, the closed-ness and closeness of the office increasingly takes on the properties of a (really big) diary or treasure chest, where children's most prized and susceptible parts of themselves can be brought and stored for safekeeping. Many children, especially those who are in turmoil, are drawn instinctively to the therapy office where their distressing feelings can be heard, explored, and put in their place.

For all of these reasons I don't conduct therapy outside my office. By doing away with that therapeutic space, we surrender much privacy and containment. While walks to the candy store can be pleasant—useful relating and discussing surely can occur during such shared activity—they compromise the therapeutic power of our work. Making the space in which we meet more open-ended risks excusing the child from much of the anxiety-provoking closeness and growth-promoting relating that propels therapy. If a little girl can discharge her discomfort by kicking a rock as she skips, or by running ahead, why would she ever stay put long enough to confront her issues and feelings? Is it a coincidence, I wonder, that child patients often request out-of-the-office field trips when they are most troubled, in trouble, or unmotivated that day to work in treatment? In some instances, going outside—for example, waiting in an ice cream store, walking through clinic hallways—simply wastes a good deal of our precious fifty minutes with the child.

Going outside can be a particularly appealing option for adolescents. Some clinicians believe that adolescents can't do therapy in a traditional office setting, that they need to be in their natural element, hanging at the hoops, for example. Yet, while appreciating the need for alternate frameworks to meet certain clinical needs, we must recognize that this option can be overused. Do we go outside because the child irretrievably lacks the resources—ego, conscience, motivation—to benefit from traditional therapy? Are we meeting the child where he is, concentrating on a more active intervention because he just could never—and I mean never—tolerate and employ talking therapy? Or do we go outside mostly to avoid our own boredom, purposely kill time, escape the discomfort of prolonged silence or confrontation? Even loudly balking teenagers, held inside for a sufficient number of sessions, can grow to use and value the intimacy and focus of therapy in the office.

The Time

What difference does it make whether we see a child for ten minutes or eighty, on Monday or every day, this week but not next? To begin with there is nothing magical about the length of the therapy session. That it approximates an hour is a matter of convenience, practicality, and clinical experience. Sessions lasting hours would be overwhelming, hard to schedule, prohibitively costly, and completely unacceptable to insurance companies. On the other hand overly abbreviated hours, much shorter than fifty minutes, make it hard for patients and therapists to settle in and get to work. Doing fifty minutes rather than a full sixty is merely our pragmatic way to make room for note-keeping, bathroom runs, and a between-sessions stretch.

And why once a week? A matter of convenience and practicality, this common arrangement is also clinically informed. Two or more sessions per week can be more of a good thing and can make for a therapy that works faster and deeper, but two are generally more than parents and health care systems are willing to underwrite. Coming less frequently than weekly, however, allows our patients to crust over, their psychic and protective shells growing back or hardening between meetings, making them less open to the therapeutic process and making each session feel much like the first.

The relative constancy of the fifty-minute hour is what carries much of the therapeutic weight.

> Mario, an extraordinarily flat and near mute 5-year-old, spent his first hour stacking dominoes into towers. He said nothing at my five-minutes-to-go warning, but he closely watched the clock advance to the final second. From the fifth session on, Mario, who worked with his back to the clock, would automatically stop within a minute of the hour's end.

Mario's internal clock was unusually sharp. All patients, however, develop their own clocks. Experiencing that regularity of time helps our patients to gauge their work. Patients often bring up certain topics at the beginning, middle, or end of an hour. Knowing when the hour ends also enables children to prepare themselves for the end, for today's goodbye, so they may regroup themselves—their wishes, longings, and pains—before leaving the sanctuary of therapy to again face life as it is. Like space, the time function also contributes to our holding patients. When a girl cries and cries at the hour's beginning, she knows she can "fall apart" for a good forty-five minutes longer; another, noting ten minutes left, sees that she'd best summarize her tale if she really wants to get to the emotional punchline. The fifty-minute set point also helps to culture and make therapeutically available issues related to separation and loss. Saying hello while knowing that good-bye comes in forty-nine minutes invokes apprehension of the end, a dread that tends to work its way toward the final minute. This measured dynamic allows the child to begin experiencing loss and related sentiments while still in the hour, while we are there to help them understand and work it through. We see evidence of this dynamic in most all of our patients whether they rush out before we dismiss them or whether they dawdle, having to draw one more leaf or suddenly feeling a need to neaten the building blocks. "What are you going to do if I don't leave," one teen threatened, "call the police?"

In a similar spirit, scheduling our patients' hours acquires meaning beyond merely coming to a time that we, they, and their parents agree to. While once-weekly therapy at any hour on any day is better than biweekly or no treatment, sameness of appointment time accentuates its potency. Knowing that 5:00 P.M. on Thursday is *their* time evokes a natural process that resembles the inner and spontaneous countdown from fifty minutes to blastoff. As children attach to the therapy process, they come to know and feel that today is the day or that the next hour is the hour. Children back from vacation will often describe with a sense of astonished curiosity their having thought of me while canoeing or playing baseball; the only connection is that I came to mind just at the time and day that we normally meet.

Having a time and day that is always theirs fosters children's sense of ownership in the treatment. While some children are able to use therapy under the most erratic and vague circumstances, a majority seem sensitive to the conditions under which they meet. Even the child who is ambivalent about therapy appreciates that one real hour in the week, of the whole 168, belongs exclusively to him, is his alone to enjoy or detest, cooperate or fight with, value or trash. The steadying effect of a child's having an established weekly hour is one of the most convincing.

These constancies in time and space demonstrate more than our words can that we take our work and this child seriously. In themselves they can be therapeutic for the child from a chaotic and unpredictable home, for instance, or the autistic child who craves orderliness. But it is our deviations from constancy that can lead to the therapeutic gold mining.

> Though I could not see him, Darren's loud sigh told me that he lay exhausted in the corner of the office. For the past forty-five minutes he'd worked furiously, using every conceivable object—blocks, gameboards, tissue boxes, seat cushions, dollhouse—to erect himself an impressive, if motley, fortress. "Could you hand me the gun?" he asked, gathering up his last ounce of strength. He pushed the gun through a hole so that it faced the office door. "Now no one can get in."
>
> Not until his cleaning up did I learn the motive for Darren's hard work and upset. "You were with other children," he blurted out. "You like them better, admit it!"

I'd only been three minutes late. But three minutes was enough for Darren to notice and read into. Like most of us, he read into that void what bothered him most: his fear that his parents loved his sister more than him, an envious worry that had come to permeate and obstruct his peer relations in school and at the playground. This agitated entry led the way for months of useful work.

When our patients come to expect us to be on time, our being tardy can take on meaning. Just as parents nervously wonder why their children haven't yet returned from school, patients wonder what's going on with us. "Did I get the wrong day?" "Is he sick? Dead?" "Is he with patients he loves more? Perhaps he's mad because of what I told him last week." "Maybe he's masturbating in the bathroom (like I do). Or maybe he's smoking a joint in there (because, like me, he can't face life without a crutch)." The ways in which patients fill the black hole of our not being there are as infinitely varied as are people.

The scale of time that prevails is partly a function of our reliability. If we tend to be punctual, our patients will start to rumble psychically within minutes. If we routinely come late, our patients will probably react less intensely and perhaps only after longer delays. While some flexibility can make schedules easier to maintain, and may superficially appear to teach children to wait and be adaptable, I think it eliminates a realm of experience that, deeply reflecting the time-limited nature of life itself, is crucial to therapy.

Our ending on time is of no less interest. Do we let sessions run on and on because the child is talking, or because he is almost finished with a skyscraper, or because he will throw an enraged tantrum should we stop him? No children like to hear that "it is time," especially when they are having fun, in the middle of some meaningful play, or feeling the comfort or glow of our being with them. But as with beginnings, endings are also interpreted by children. "Did my therapist let me stay an extra 10 minutes because I was a good girl?" "Did she let me stay because she is afraid of my explosions, and afraid that I'll make an even noisier scene in the waiting room and really throw off her schedule?" Or "How come she was so relaxed about my leaving last week but today she wants me out pronto? She must like me less this week."

I'm not suggesting that we need to live by atomic clocks that lose less than a second in our lifetime. I am instead praising the value of reasonable consistency, for without it we are left to measure what is happening in the relationship with a yardstick made of elastic. Moreover, unreliability in ourselves diminishes our right and incentive to recognize it in our patients. Clinicians who have trouble with punctuality are prone to dismiss their patients'. How can we, in good conscience, confront a teenager's frequent lateness if we are equally tardy?

We expect children, often via their parents, to show up for their appointments each week. If a child is not coming regularly, we need to assess whether she is even in treatment. To mistake one or two initial meetings followed by months of cancellations and no-shows for therapy is self-deceiving and dangerous. We, the child and family, are better off recognizing what is and taking reasonable action. I make clear from the onset that missed sessions and last-minute cancellations (with no good excuse) will be charged for. This condition is not to make me easy money; it gives parents a needed push when they are feeling tired, overwhelmed, or ambivalent about therapy. (I realize that some insurance, clinic, and public assistance policies do not allow clinicians to do this.)

When committing to a therapy, we too make an agreement to be there. If we cancel sessions at whim, how can we expect a child or parent to see the work as an earnest enterprise? How can we tell Jane's parents that her suffering warrants treatment, but then cancel her sessions in the second and sometimes fourth week of every month?

Limits

There aren't a whole lot of rules in relationship-based play and talk therapy. Although we hope that children will play and talk freely, the golden rule of analysis—to say (or try to say) whatever comes to mind—doesn't apply here so purely. Sometimes, like analysts, we sit back and watch our patients follow their hearts and unconscious, playing at will and with ease until their own internal conflicts and inhibitions get in the way. More commonly, children do not agree to therapy the way grownups sign on for psychoanalysis. And their therapies in most instances involve much more tangible involvement with their therapists. We do, however, ask as a basic rule that they be as honest as they can with themselves and us.

Believing it is the shortest route to where we need to go, we try to follow our patients' leads as unobtrusively as we can, interfering only as we must. Rather than listing all the ways that are permitted and all the ways that are not, we wait and see, holding back our intervening until their actions or words call for it. Children being human and children, however, they inevitably want to know what is expected of them. Struggling to define themselves in this context of ambiguity and competing demands (coincidentally, a task that looks a lot like growing up), they test us and the process, sometimes like crazy.

Why don't we simply state what is and isn't okay, or if the list is too long, offer a printed handbook that describes the actions and language that are forbidden in the therapy room? To begin a relationship that way surely would convey a tone of authority and oppression that would do anything but foster the open and accepting atmosphere we intend. Who of us would choose to dine at a restaurant whose menu's third page listed "no talking with your mouth open," "spoons are to be used only for soup," "no elbows on the table"? Furthermore, using the shotgun method to scatter a ton of prohibitive buckshot would make each child who enters our doors feel like every other child, likely offending children who would never consider doing everything naughty on that list (which means just about every child). Primarily, though, by defining what can and can't happen up front robs children of the opportunity to make that discovery themselves, on their own terms and in their own time. Frankly, children tend to know pretty well what can and can't be done without being told. Rather than prematurely imposing structure or cutting off misbehaving alleys, we rely on limits after the fact or as the fact is making itself known. But for that matter, what is the purpose of setting limits at all?

For one thing, children can't be allowed to hurt themselves or their therapists. It's not hard to grasp why a therapist can't permit child patients to hit him on the head whenever they're frustrated. But even milder assaults are unacceptable for they imply that hitting or some aggressive variant is an okay way to express frustration. Hurting their therapist can lead children to feel intolerable guilt or hypervigilant fear that the therapist will get them back—by hurting them or telling their parents—when their guard is down.

When I entered the office, Bethany, as was her custom, jumped out from behind the door to surprise me, banging me in the face with an armful of toys, as she'd also done before.

Recognizing that her exuberant greetings held much affection as well as hostility, I nonetheless set a limit on Bethany's going into the office before me. Having tried in vain to set earlier limits ("You can jump but not with toys in your arms"), stopping the jumping completely was my only choice. Although Bethany was not hurting me badly, the weekly whack on my nose and occasional poke in the eye were making me like her less. My limit served less to protect me physically and more to protect my good feeling for her so that I might continue, as Ginott wrote, "to maintain [my] attitudes of acceptance, empathy and regard" for her (1959, p. 161).

We also don't allow our child patients to harm themselves, though this can be a tricky path to hoe.

Victor had a long history of self-destructive behavior prior to his therapy with me. Now, months into treatment, feeling more comfortable with me, he began showing me his more anguished impulses to harm himself. On his forearms he'd write hateful epitaphs to himself, occasionally pushing the pen hard enough to jab the skin. When the dull children's scissors failed to cut his bangs, he simply tugged the jammed scissors, pulling hair out. However, when he inserted the point of an unbent paper clip up his nose, drawing blood, I set a limit.

Why, a reasonable reader may wonder, did I wait so long to do something? Consider Victor. According to his parents, his own and previous therapists' reports, he'd treated himself poorly for years, twice expressing suicidal gestures. Whether in mild self-mutilating or more indirectly, with daredevil behavior and drug experimenting, he showed a wish to harm himself. What were my choices? I could, as did an earlier therapist, push to hospitalize him, but for what purpose? That would do little more, I thought, than buy me some time, putting off the clinical hardship that had to be faced. Alternatively, I could set a limit, refusing to treat him whenever he did anything slightly resembling a self-hurting act. But I am not so full of my clinical self to believe that my withholding would inspire his self-control and self-analysis of his inner torment. Rather than corner him into healthier behavior I would likely leave him feeling abandoned and alone with his toxic impulses.

And so, as therapists often do, I tried to accompany him down the narrow path that lay between his caring self and the self that sought to destroy him. When he displayed behaviors on the margin of self-harm, I watched carefully, wondering aloud what was driving him at that precise moment. Usually, we'd find a small insight, such as his feeling like "a piece of shit" because he couldn't play a certain measure of a Jimi Hendrix song.

But when he took actions that seemed more sharply hurtful, such as stabbing the inside of his nose, he also grew less open to verbalizing what it might mean. Seeing that he now was more intent on hurting than understanding himself, I set the limit, refusing to talk further with him until he was ready to do some therapy. The positive leverage accrued by my having stayed with him through a majority of his self-tweaking acts up to that hour helped to bring him back to work in minutes. Limits helped me to keep Victor safe enough, if on the edge, so that we could ultimately learn what had been fueling his extraordinary shame and self-hatred.

Children's testing of us frequently gauges how much aggression we will tolerate. "Can we hit you?" (No.) "Can we push you against the wall?" (No.) "Can we spit in your coffee cup?" (No.) "Can we deliberately ruin your toys?" (No, though under some circumstances—for example, with a child who is being sadistically hurtful of others or one who is severely inhibited—I do allow the torture of a specific toy to the point of its destruction.) "Can we attack your other patients as we leave the office?" (No.) "Can we shoot your Nerf blaster?" (Yes, that's why it's here.) "Can we shoot it at your face?" (No.) "How about at your butt?" (No.) "Can we at least shoot the side of your foot?" (No, because that's still part of me and you know it.) "Can we shoot my mother who's in the waiting room?" (No. While I generally leave parents to do their own disciplining in my presence, I do not allow my toy guns to be shot at other people.) "Can we shoot your pictures?" (No, they are covered with glass.) "Can we shoot your toy figures, your walls, your desk, your chair, and everything else in here that speaks of you?" (Yes, you can shoot anything that's not breakable.) Their exasperated begging and demands to shoot us testify to the strength of their wish that we respond to their provocation, and the strength of their craving for limits.

In addition to keeping us, them, and the therapy safe, we have even better reasons to set limits on the aggression aimed our way. By not letting children do whatever they might with us, we challenge their ego to contain the hostility, withstand the frustration, and delay gratification of the impulse. We let them know, however, that they can express their aggression verbally. Put it into words, we encourage them, knowing that they need the exercise of putting feelings into words more than they need a human punching bag. By controlling their aggression here and there, bit by bit, children grow more able to manage it constructively and to assert themselves verbally.

I have no problem with children screaming at me, calling me this or that, teasing me, or sharing their fantasies of how they would love to torture me. After all, though sticks and stones can break our bones, we know better about names. Most of the time I find that this behavior passes easily, clearing the way for some useful exploration of its meaning. However, cases in which this putting down doesn't let up, running for every minute of every hour, tell me that this purging of venom on and into me, while relieving, is therapeutically not doing much and must be checked.

Limits comparably apply to children's expressions of sexuality and affection. For the most part, children's fondness for us is generally a good thing and shows itself throughout many therapies. They make us gifts and heart-shaped "love you" cards. They lean against us when telling their story or rest their foot on ours while drawing at the desk. And some give us hugs on their way in or out of the hour. What could these kind and sweet gestures possibly have to do with limits?

For some children their wish to love us and be loved back grows excessive. They insatiably want hugs upon hugs or hugs that turn into kisses and more. Giving them that love is likely to confuse them, for we meet, not to physically love them, but to do the talking and playing work of therapy. "Why," a child may wonder, "does my therapist hug me when I am sad but not when I am angry?" "Why am I getting love today but not in last week's session?" Doesn't our gratifying the wish for our love and consolation risk detouring the therapeutic process? While a girl who is frightened may want my arms around her, she will benefit much more from my psychically holding her while we together try to understand her great fear and sudden need for my all-protectiveness.

Children's requests for affection often, if not always, relate to some psychological impetus. Children who incessantly and from day one shower me with love often do so not out of admiration, but out of dread, their love meant to appease me and ward off the danger they perceive coming from adults or to feed what they may imagine to be my narcissism. Those children who beg and plead for my affection toward them are often riddled with insecurity about whether they are loved and lovable. In neither instance would my giving affection substantially solve their problems, soothe their longing, or resolve the larger underlying issue.

We must be particularly prudent about our physical closeness with children who have been sexually abused. Their trauma experiences may propel them to push for our physical affection. But our giving it would surely do more harm than good. Gently declining their appeals, we help them instead to understand why they so want us to love them that way: "Because we are frightened that sooner or later you are going to rape us anyway." "Because we only get love and attention at home when we act sexy." "Because that is what being loved by a daddy means to me."

Limits, while seeming to halt the child, paradoxically can move her ahead on her therapeutic mission. Consider a murderously rageful child who zings a paper plane at my face. What would happen if I should take a hands-off approach and say or do nothing in response? Well, the shock of seeing his plane jab my eye might be enough to shock a boy and evoke remorse, and the resulting guilt might possibly block his continuing to work on the anger he feels for a divorced father who forgot his birthday. Excited by his having hurt me, a second and less socialized boy might raise the ante, pelting me with dominoes, then markers, and finally large wooden blocks, again bringing the therapy to a dead end.

By setting a limit on a boy's aggression toward me and diverting it to a more symbolic realm, however, the play and impulses beneath can go to their full and rich expression. "It's not okay to throw planes at me, but you can throw planes at this little me," I say, grabbing a small play figure and setting it on the desk. In fact, that boy will soon see for himself that he can do virtually anything he wants to that plastic Dr. Bromfield. He can step on me, roll me in the mud, knock me down, abuse me, torture me, put me in his pocket, or even kill and bury me. Setting a limit and redirecting the play into a safer mode applies equally to matters of affection and sexuality. "You can't sleep with me but you [or the plastic figure that is you] can do whatever you want with this Dr. Bromfield [figure]." On both fronts the scenarios that children come up with are endless, and take their play and thoughts to a more complete resolution than would physically using me as a real object of their hostility and desires.

Limits also serve to give our patients a needed place in therapy, no less than in the home, to express the childhood hurts that are too big and painful to bring up directly.

"That's it," I said, having stated clearly that drawing on the wall would not be tolerated. I put the markers in my desk drawer.

"You don't let me do anything," Anna screamed. "But you let everyone else do they want! You don't care if the other kids draw on your walls. Only me," she went on through her angry tears. "I'm the only one you hate."

Naive bystanders, and many a parent, might think that Anna was overreacting to my not letting her draw on my wall. If that was all she was responding to, they would be right. But she was feeling much more. Her divorced mother had recently remarried, and Anna was justified in feeling left out. Her 56-year-old father had more interest in his own grandchildren, and her mother, infatuated with her new love, was much less available. "What about me?" Anna eventually asked me, herself, and her mother. My limit gave Anna, who was originally unable to broach the topic herself, a hook on which to hang her resentment, a legitimate place to begin venting her much broader distress.

Having established the power and necessity of limits, we should think about how to use them. They work best when administered matter-of-factly and with assurances, not when we are red with anger or at our wit's end. And they tend to work best when applied early, that is, when the child is better able to control herself. I do not wait to be hit on the head with a hammer. I set a limit when the child simply pokes me in the hand with a nail.

Whether or not we set a limit depends enormously on the nature of the individual child in the context. If a seriously well-behaved but inhibited child finally throws a lifesaver at me—a sign of his progress in treatment—I do nothing but help him to struggle with the guilt-laden aftermath of his act. However, when an impulsive child does the same, as happens more frequently, I set an immediate limit. If he continues, I simply end the session for that day. Even if full of hostility, children who are attached to me and the therapy do not like being thrown out.

We also try to set limits empathically. I know that, however clinically correct, stopping a patient from hiding under my shirt feels like rejection by someone he dearly loves and values. And so, after setting the limit, I stay open to the hurt and resentment I've caused as well as to note and accept the "I'm going to hate you back" retaliation that's apt to show up in the talk and play that follows.

As with any other intervention the more judiciously limits are used, the more effectively they work. We aspire to set limits that are in a child's best interest or that are in some other way clinically necessary. Our imposing limits sadistically or punitively, perhaps acting out some dislike of the child, anger at her parents or frustration over her lack of progress, only hurts the treatment. Some therapists shy away from limits; others run to them too eagerly. The best we can do is strive to know our own style of setting limits, paying close attention to when they work and when they don't, making sure to clean up any fallout they produce.

Confidentiality

The issue of confidentiality is basic. While some clinicians suggest complex explanations and preparation, I think the surest way for children to grasp the matter is by our demonstrating it. Each week they share with us, and each week that we don't betray that trust persuades our child patients that we can keep what they say and do just between the two of us. This secure arrangement helps to hold the therapy and allies with the child's own willingness to reveal and examine herself. Why would children tell me something if they know I might turn around and tell their parents?

Our keeping what is in therapy safe from the outside world—isn't that essentially what confidentiality does?—also highlights for children our view that they run their own therapy, that they are responsible for its work. It also stresses the need for their honesty. As long as I can rely on a child's accounting of what goes on in his life, the less I look to those on the outside for confirmation or accurate lowdown. Confidentiality is an aspect of the honor system that exists between us and our child patients when we both keep our end of the therapeutic bargain.

I don't make a big deal of integrating data that comes from outside of therapy, mainly from parents and schools. I encourage parents to keep me informed and let children know that this two-way street of communication exists. I shy away from the deep-throat approach to informing. It is hard to make good use of information that comes to me with requests to keep the source anonymous. If the school says that Aries is disrupting the class, I need to be able to tell her how I know of this in order to help her. Seldom does keeping this type of secret enhance therapy. Moreover, children will catch the drift that I and their parents or teachers are sneaking behind their backs, which can gravely disrupt the therapeutic trust.

For parent updates of their child's treatment, I can generally describe what is going on without giving away the specifics of their play or words. When I need to include the parents in something more pressing, I try always to speak first with the child, enlisting her help concerning the best way to break the news to a parent. Or I may simply invite the parents in, sharing what I have to say in general terms, leaving child and parents to fill in the blanks. In those rare instances where I must talk with the parents without the child's cooperation, I find that my upfront admission that I will be breaking confidentiality and spelling out my candid reasons for doing so usually lead to an acceptance and understanding that what I have done came out of caring and my best effort to do right by the child.

This matter of confidentiality raises the bigger question of the child therapist's ethics, a matter that acquires even greater significance in the contemporary context of shrinking insurance and health plan support for mental health services. After all, it's easy to do the right thing when the right thing is also the quickest, smoothest, and most well-paying. Unfortunately, real-world clinical choices seldom look like that. *Ethics* means to do what we think is best and clinically right, even when doing so means clinically working harder, confronting more difficult situations or feelings, getting lesser rewards, or bucking popular opinion (including the parents' and school's). That we do much of it in such an isolated and unstructured realm only adds import to the big and little decisions we make on behalf of our patients and their therapies.

5

TELL ME WHERE IT HURTS: ON TALKING AND QUERYING

Words are the currency of therapeutic change. While much takes place in the physical and psychic space between us and our patients, it is our and their words that most tell each other what is happening. What specific functions do our words serve and how do we best apply them clinically?

Probably the most obvious function of what we say is to promote our learning more about the child. For some specific information we simply ask direct questions. "How old are you?" "What grade are you in?" "Do you have any brothers or sisters?" Although such sharp queries grow tiresome, they have their place in treatment. Beginning patients can appreciate a forewarning that we will be asking a lot of questions early on but that we'll ask many fewer as we get to know them better.

But such close-ended questions tend to elicit close-ended answers—like "no," "yeah," "3," "seventh grade," "never"—that tell us little and put us in the position of having to ask a follow-up question, and another, then another, forcing us to make nags of ourselves. Wanting to give us the pithy answers we seem to ask for, even cooperative and talkative children tend to respond minimally. In contrast, open-ended queries do not invite quick and easy answers. "Do you like school?" limits what a child can say and implies that any reply but yes is a wrong one. But "what's school like for you?" asks for all of the child's impressions, however big, small, many, positive, negative, or ambivalent.

According to one of the paradoxes that characterize human behavior, children tend to talk more to adults who ask less. And open-ended declarative statements seem to invite even more response than do open-ended questions. "You're at the new high school." "You've got a little sister." "It's a beautiful sunny day and you had to come here." Children tend to respond most willingly and fully to these questions hidden in statements, as if they are most open to telling when they think we are least wanting and asking them to.

This variant of the need to oppose us and our demands reflects, I think, their reading our less directed questioning to mean less ill motives on our part. Questions typically arouse suspicion, causing us to wonder why someone wants to know and what they intend to do with this information. Guardedness leads to shorter, sparser, more defensive replies. Children frequently are so accustomed to parents' high-speed whats, whens, and whys that they readily note and appreciate our more respectful and minimally intrusive manner. They sense rightly that our calmer query is meant to stoke a discussion more than to collect enough evidence to indict them.

Of course, how we ask questions influences the kinds of answers we get. "Oh, you're at Jefferson? You love it there, right? Doesn't everybody?" When we ask, do we allow enough time for the child to reply before going to our follow-up? Well, if Andrea doesn't downright love that school, would she even bother telling us after all that? Being peppered with questions can make children feel attacked or give them the sense that we are mechanically going down a laundry list and don't really care what they answer.

How we react verbally to what children say contributes to our creating an open atmosphere in which our child patients want to talk. When children tell us what they think and feel, do we respond with anger, criticism, or rejection? If so, we risk teaching children to keep themselves to themselves. Are we able to sit still and hear the whole story without jumping to conclusions or taking panicked action?

Therapy, being a self-exploration, requires that patients tell their stories. We try our best to let them do so as much as they can on their own. When they flounder about in their tales, the urge to help organize them is great. Just as it is to complete their sentences or to jump in with the words they can't find. Children likely will take what we give, sometimes even with seeming appreciation. But our interrupting implies that we have neither the patience nor the willingness to wait for them to talk for themselves. There's also a good chance that what we fill in the blanks is not what they would have said if left on their own. When a child, overwhelmed by too much to tell, asks me where to start, I tend to put her in charge. "Wherever you think you should," I patiently answer, certain that her choice will be both best and revealing.

In the same spirit I do not feign understanding, for example, laughing at a joke I do not get or showing sympathy when I can't see the hurt. I frequently ask children to explain a situation again or to repeat what I was unable to hear clearly. Should their reasoning fail me, I ask for their help. "I'm sorry. You're trying to help me see how your mom's birthday caused your fight at soccer practice. But I'm still not getting it. Can you try again?" When I admit my not getting it, and acknowledge their efforts, most children are quite willing to persist. If they feel that we don't care enough to pursue them, or that we blame them for our not understanding, they will often let the matter go and pull back a bit from therapy. Our overeagerness to oblige their "Never mind, it's no big deal" un-wittingly says to them, "You're right. It's no big deal and certainly not worth any more of this effort."

Assuming that we want our child patients to understand us and we want to understand them, we strive to speak in ways to match their cognitive and development levels. Do we use words and syntax that they can understand? "You've experienced a great loss," while suiting an adolescent, would fly over most toddlers' heads, leaving them that much more alone with their feelings. Do we use ninety-seven–word sentences burdened with big words and psychological jargon that numb rather than touch our patients? Do we use complicated sentences, employing several if–then kinds of clauses or triple negatives that, instead of clarifying, tie a child's mind into knots? Is our logic too beyond, or beneath, the child's? Do we use irony or subtlety more fitting a literate and psychologically minded adult than a 9-year-old child with low average intelligence?

While experience and (clinical) practice tend to make us better at speaking to the child's level, we also have the resources to observe the effects of our words. Children's glazed expressions, complete changing of subjects, wholly unrelated responses or more explicit "huhs?" and the like can tip us off that we are not making ourselves clear. Just as we persist in urging a child to get us to understand, we push ourselves to try again, asking where we lost him, and making sure he knows that the problem in communicating is with us.

What kind of language is acceptable in the therapy hour? For children, any they wish to use. After all, who knows better than they what words they need to express themselves? This doesn't mean we don't heed or probe the words they use. "What does that mean?" I have asked, with a smile, of a child who simply and defensively says that "school sucks." We could ask children who swear with every other word not to, but to what end? To become just another arm of the parental authority, confirming all their worst fears about therapy and us? Far more can be got out of listening intently when they brave a longer and curseless phrase, rewarding them for that risk-taking, implicitly encouraging them to talk like that more often.

I tend to curse little in the hour myself, particularly with children who do so a lot. Yet, while sharing their street language may seem to be a good route to connection, I wonder if I don't cheapen the therapy when I ally more with their protective, belittling stance against self-examination and growth. I have not met one adolescent who has found my "cleaner" language either offensive, distressing, or off-putting. They seem to pay me back for my respect of their language with a respect for my own. I am more apt to curse with an inhibited child who struggles to make his frustrations and anger known because curse words carry so much more vitality when used sparingly.

Our language also is key in our establishing and maintaining an empathic attitude. How do we signal children that we are listening and know what they mean? We can reflect what they say to us, showing that we grasp it. "You're so frustrated with math homework." "No one believes you." "Coming to therapy feels like punishment." Our verbal restating underlines for us and our patients what they have said, showing them that we now know, or giving them the opportunity to correct our perceptions or clarify what they meant. Speaking in this reflecting manner can feel quite awkward to beginning therapists, for few of us talk this way in normal conversation. When first attempting to do so, therapists may imagine their patients responding with "So, what? That's what I just said." And, if applied too often, too mechanically, and without true understanding, such remarks will strike patients as lame, robotic, and insincere. As with most interventions, our reflecting works best when used discreetly and at the proper moments, when we really want to confirm and emphasize an important thought or feeling.

We might also ask ourselves why we sometimes use such extended psychobabble to convey simple matters. Is it for our own or our patients' good? "You're feeling as if adults sometimes don't treat you with as much respect as you feel you deserve?" is a lot more tentative and circumspect than "You didn't like my asking your mother about your report card." The former and more distanced phrasing might well serve a fragile girl who can't tolerate a more direct stating of her upset with me; on the other hand, the latter might feel more empathic and real to a second girl who is closer to and more able to acknowledge her rage.

"That stinks." "What nonsense." "You're dying and I don't care." "You hate me and therapy." "What's the point of living?" Such short and pithy phrases, while sounding harsh out of context, might most acutely resonate with the vivid feelings of our patients. Our caring efforts not to overwhelm our patients can lead us to weak speech that doesn't take emotional stands and leaves children feeling cold and alone.

Our discomfort with what the child is saying, especially about us, can deter our best attempts to empathize. Empathizing with a child's love for us ("You want me to have your flowers") is easier than getting in touch with her pure hatred and wish to destroy us ("You wish I was dead and gone"). Each of us has different vulnerabilities—involving aggression, sexuality, love, loss, or any other aspect of human experience—that we carry into our work as therapists. Our changing the subject or raising the level of discussion might, if we look, be an attempt to escape something that hurts, stresses, or repulses us. What really motivates our querying about homework when a girl talks of her smelly brown diarrhea? If we sidetrack her with our preferred interest, we will miss hers (in that case, a wish to smear my office walls with feces).

Sometimes we intend our interpreting to make what is unconscious conscious. Bringing conflict or hurt to awareness allows children to see what is actually transpiring within them, allowing them to know what is distressing them so—sometimes enabling them to then make decisions about what they wish to do about it, if anything.

Lenny, a high school sophomore, was a good hockey player but he could have been stellar. He was also a good piano student who his teacher felt had the talent to be exceptional. Despite superior aptitude, he was a mediocre student in school, where he was exceedingly well liked by his teachers and peers. Lenny claimed that he liked how he was doing just fine and belittled his parents' and teachers' concern for him. Yet he came to therapy quite willingly and dependably. When here he frequently told of dreams in which he was unable to perform: given a test that was written in Chinese, being unable to put the puck into an open goal, finding that his recital piano had no keys. He perpetually spoke with longing admiration for those achieving more than he.

In about the fifth month, with little apparent change at school or home, Lenny described with upset a nightmare that had troubled him even more than usual. In this dream, having been elected captain for his team's championship game, he was about to be the hero. With seconds remaining, the score tied 0–0, Lenny all alone pouring down on the opposing goalie, the blades fell off his skates. Determined to overcome this mishap, Lenny kept skating until, inches from the goal and certain victory, he shot—but the blade of his stick broke off and the puck slid harmlessly to the boards. Lenny woke up in tears, not knowing how the game turned out.

"That's the story of my life," Lenny said with a regret I'd never heard him speak directly. Seeing that he continued to be distressed, I asked whether there was more to the dream but Lenny shook his head no. My gentle queries about various parts of the dream fell flat until I asked whether anyone had come to see him play. With a torrent of feeling and tears that blindsided him, Lenny recalled looking up from the ice, just before his skates disintegrated, to see his father's wheelchair rolling out of control down the Boston Garden's steep stairway. "Who gives a crap about a hockey game," he cried, "when your father's about to croak?"

A loving and good son, Lenny always had known how sad he was that his father had been paralyzed in a car accident. But he had never been able to see ways in which he was angry about having lost his father's physical involvement in his life. Nor had he recognized the guilt he felt about not being paralyzed, about being able to achieve and triumph beyond what his father could ever be able to do. By gaining awareness of his self-castrating way of coping— after all, wasn't it Lenny who held back his pursuits and who, in his dreams, would shoot himself in his own foot?—Lenny was able to more directly grieve his father's condition and go on with his life more fully. This freeing up, not so coincidentally, brought Lenny closer to his father and more able to see the ways in which his quite active father could still be a presence in his life. By coming to see what really bothered him, Lenny no longer needed to destroy his life or himself in effigy.

Though I do not do child analysis, I regularly find that the big repressed experiences and impulses can wreak the most havoc in children: hatred and sadism in inhibited children, yearnings for love and dependency in those who are habitually aggressive, homophobic dread in adolescents. However, unearthing these can be as arduous and dirty as excavating buried treasure.

That some experiences are repressed, put out of consciousness, is the most conspicuous testimony to their threatening vigor. The more potentially toxic to the psyche, the more deeply they're hidden. But they can't be quickly uprooted or cut out like a nasty tumor for they are not discrete things.

Clinical tradition, meaning the wisdom from experience, has taught us the need to respect the way children have come to adapt to their stresses. "You're a frightened little boy with a tiny penis and no mommy," while expressing the psychological truth a 15-year-old near-delinquent boy feels inside, would probably scare him off from therapy. Instead, we work gradually toward the ultimate revelation. "You've got to be macho at Roosevelt," recognizing his tough guy defense. "You can't let your guard down," recognizing his mistrust. "You don't need anyone but you," recognizing his inability to rely on others. And so we go, each comment and its digestion peeling off a layer, growing closer to the stronger and more noxious core.

While quicker and more piercing interpretations can occasionally bring miraculous results, they generally go nowhere or, more usually in my experience, send the child reeling. The most useful comments address unconscious material that is just a translucent layer below the surface. That is why remarks we make today can have so much more impact than the same remarks made yesterday or last year.

Because so much is unknown, mixed up, and not yet understood, our task can be a challenging one. How do we comment, or interpret, in ways that tap what can be tapped, confirm what can be confirmed, console and confront, while reaching all levels of a conflict—doing all in a way that can be tolerated, grasped, and gainfully used by the child? The easiest way is by taking the time to consider all that the child says in an hour.

Alicia was frustrated beyond belief. Her parents always seemed to be faulting her. Her teachers picked on her. Her once beloved grandmother was turning on her. Her boyfriend was a selfish pig. Her friends betrayed her. She had a headache. School was too hard. School was too easy. Her new shoes hurt. "Why," she asked, "did you get such a bad haircut?" For pretty much fifty minutes Alicia complained about most everything and everybody in the world.

Although Alicia brought up dozens of issues that caught my interest, I did not probe any of them. I sat back and let her run her course. Rather than feeling the need to show meaning here, there, and everywhere, I save my interpretive arrows for the most opportune moments. Wanting to say something, I decided to go over in time, in what was actually a fifty-third or fifty-fourth minute, and wondered aloud, "Why doesn't anyone love me?" This rather simple comment, almost too obvious to say and spoken directly by me in the first person, brought a flood of tears and subsequent weeks of discussion about the ways she mistreated those in her life.

Since what children express often reflects dynamics operating on a larger and deeper scale inside, we may want to make comments that simultaneously access the superficial and deep: consider a child who literally erased the stick figure of me she'd drawn, reflecting a guilt-ridden and conflicted wish to kill the uncle who'd molested her. In a manner that she could tolerate, my remarking,

"You want to erase me away," confirmed the visible tip of a much larger and sinister iceberg, her wish to lethally erase her uncle. To have interpreted more directly her wish to kill the man would have overwhelmed her and reinforced her undeserved but nonetheless guilt-ridden conviction that the abuse was her fault.

Almost any therapy worth its salt would reveal a therapist and patient having together developed a common language by which to communicate. Whether it is in the nuance, the rhythm, the specific words—be they typical, slang, or made-up—or even in the shared jokes, we create a cultural context specific to that therapy and child. For example, one boy early in the treatment ended a lengthy and belabored discussion of his wayward behavior by noting that sometimes he can just plain be a "rat's ass." For the remainder of his treatment his exclaiming "rat's ass" became a shorthand signal that he'd screwed up and needed to fess up to what he'd done.

This evolution of a shared language serves two purposes. First, it allows us to share information, both factual and emotional. Most child patients find talking to their therapist easier over time. Second, that language, known only to the two of us, therapist and child, acquires a specialness, propelling the therapeutic attachment while paralleling that between mother and child. Children prefer using this language to spelling out their complicated situations, thoughts, and feelings for they'd rather that we, like all powerful mothers, just know all that they feel and need without having to ask, without confronting their separateness.

Since speaking what is in their minds and hearts is a basic demand of their work with us, therapy constantly exercises children's capacity to put thoughts and feelings into words. Our limits further tell them that their impulse to action must be expressed in the form of play, or perhaps even better, in the form of language. And so, in the course of their therapy, many children grow more accustomed and better able to express themselves verbally. Instead of hitting, they can speak of their wish to hit; instead of cheating, they can speak of their wish to cheat; instead of withdrawing and rejecting, they can speak of their wish to withdraw and reject. For children who rely on their headaches and other bodily pains to speak for their conflicts, putting their feelings into words, particularly within an interpersonal relationship, can reduce the stressful toll their conflicts place on their bodies.

Our comments are also often intended to note discrepancies that our child patients are unaware of.

> "You say you don't need anybody, but you depend on your mother to do your homework, pack your backpack, get your clothes together, give you every penny you spend, and do almost everything else that other 16-year-olds do for themselves."
>
> Though Derek didn't like what I said, he recognized its validity just as he recognized my having waited many months to speak out. Rather than argue my point piece by piece, week by week, and forcing him into a corner, I held on until Derek himself seemed close to seeing the contradiction between his behavior and words. I was leery of making him feel ridiculed or put down. What he heard was my observing that his weekly tirades concerning his utter self-sufficiency were self-deceptive. This contrast led him to begin a successful examining of why growing up frightened him.

Although it's tempting to hammer our patients on their heads with the contradictions we see in their beliefs and behaviors, such quick and heavy-handed tactics generally do little good and risk deterring the development of a strong working alliance. We tend to go faster by going slowly, by confronting gently and in due time. Rather than accuse Derek, "Who are you kidding? You're the biggest baby of them all!" I spoke in a more compassionate spirit that said, "I'm confused. You speak of independence and yet consistently seek its opposite. What does this profound and enduring irony mean for your life and how you live it?"

This nonthreatening confrontation follows our relatively neutral attitude toward our patients' conflicts. When Kyle was terrified about water and his father wanted him to be a weekend sailor, I had to remain equidistant from both extremes. Otherwise, like his father, I would have been prone to push him toward the sea, or, conversely, I would have fueled his phobia, scaring him off from something, the sailing, that he himself wanted despite his anxiety. As another example, when a boy tells me about his mistreating the family cat, criticizing or endorsing his actions would be obstructive. "Why does he need to hurt innocent animals?" is my burning question. The more open I am to both sides of the conflict, both sides of an ambivalence, the more will I and my child patient learn about its meaning. Only when the child himself sees the reasons for what he does—"My mother loves that damn cat more than me"—will my vote for more humane treatment of pets make an impact.

Whatever our patients' dilemma—"Should I belittle my annoying sister?" "Should I disrupt the class?" "Should I forgive my unavailable father?" "Should I experiment sexually?" "Should I try out for the drama club?" "Should I go to that faraway private college or the local state school?"—we help most by inquiring about all aspects, particularly those we disapprove of or can't understand. By doing so we enable children to realize more clearly what they are thinking, feeling, and experiencing. We can push all we want, but only when Julie herself finally sees that she can be selfish to others, and admits that she hates that about herself, can we usefully take the next step to ask what she wants to do to resolve matters.

Should a child claim that she *can't* [fill in the blank], I almost routinely reply, "You *can't* or you *won't?*" I've yet to meet one child who does not know the difference. By our and our child patients' approaching this question seriously, we find out where best to go. True instances of *I can't* call for empathic support for children's helplessness and their predicament; those of *I won't*—including the cases in which a strong measure of won't mixes with can't—require more of a mutual press to know why.

Just as our and the child's talk is significant, so are the silences. These common periods where words do not come must be treated with the same respect and interest as those full of dialogue. What do they mean? Having told a longwinded or stressful tale, has a child run out of things to say or the energy to say them? Is that narcissistically fragile girl not talking because she saw us squelch a yawn, a sure sign to her that we are no longer interested in her? Children sometimes don't talk out of shyness, embarrassment, fear of ridicule, anger, to be oppositional, and, most of all, because they may not want us or themselves to hear and know something about them.

Where does the silence come from? I am less struck by the silence of a child who is habitually a man of few words than that of a talkative child who, while telling of his mother's walking out on his father, suddenly falls mute. "What is it?" I am prone to ask a child whose quietness is seeming to be pregnant with meaning, particularly hurt. When first hearing this question, children (and adults) nearly always have to ask what I mean, and note the oddity of my words. However, after learning that I mean, "Why have you grown silent at this exact moment?"—and experiencing that as something legitimate to wonder about—that phrase becomes a powerful and useful tool for the remainder of the treatment.

My asking, "What is it?"—especially when posed in a period of obvious distress—often evokes tears and other forms of intense affect. This finding underlines the need for therapists to leave room for silences to flourish and ripen. Patients can rush to fill in silences so as to avoid their discomfort and the revelations they can bring; therapists often cut off silences, too, for similar reasons. Many conflicts, and their associated pains, require the stress and emptiness of a silence in which to bubble up. Sitting for an extended period of time in silence, however, can be hard for therapists, stirring up their own anguish as well as taxing them with feelings of helplessness or inactivity.

Being human, we continually have thoughts and feelings in our work with children. Many of these inner sensations tell us more about ourselves than our patients, and are not to be shared aloud with them. Many others, while providing clues to the therapy, serve best by silently informing us and our interventions. As a general rule, by trying to speak only when we have something useful or helpful to say, not when we are anxious or pressured to talk, we preserve the power of our voice for the times we do talk, and ensure that we leave plenty of room for the child's needed reflecting, feeling, and being alone with us.

II

TECHNIQUES
AND TOOLS

6

THE LOWDOWN ON HIGH DRAMA: PLAYING WITH PUPPETS AND ACTION FIGURES

Puppet play can be fun, and the attentions of a responsive adult can be pleasurable. However, as is true for play therapy in general, the major purpose of puppet play is not to entertain the child or the therapist. Puppet play is nothing more than a vehicle to expedite the attaining of treatment goals, be they changed behaviors, symptom relief, self-understanding, or the freedom to be who one is. Puppets and action figures, found in almost every playroom, are frequently taken for granted. What purposes do they serve? And how can we help our child patients use them to the most therapeutic advantage?

Arguably, of all their many and important functions, dolls and action figures—the latter essentially being dolls for boys—serve to place conflict and other unwanted psychic stuff outside the child. Such exteriorizing is the most natural of human activities in the same way that we are apt to blame others when we mess up or can't find the keys, or as seen in the ease which most of us can see our own faults in others. While a lifetime of such disavowal makes for troubled and trouble-causing individuals, such externalizing within the context of therapy is an understandable defense against impulses, experiences, and truths that hurt too much to take on as one's own.

Puppets allow the child to more safely express feelings that are meant for or were originally connected to real people, be they others or themselves, or parts of people. This displacing helps to ensure greater physical and psychological safety, which invites greater self-expression.

> "Here, have some more. Come on, you love it, don't you! Have some more." Jenna, an extraordinarily reserved and compliant 7-year-old referred for severe headaches with no apparent physical cause, cruelly rammed the plastic bottle into the small dog puppet's mouth. "There you go," Jenna continued, pushing the plastic nipple so hard she hurt her hand inside the puppet. "Drink all your vodka. That's a good baby."

Jenna was furious over years of neglect by her alcoholic mother. In play, she did to the puppet what she could not do to her mother in real life for fear that her mother would retaliate and, even more, that she'd hurt her mother's feelings. Our shared perception that Jenna's puppet play, however earnest, was make-believe encouraged her to reveal feelings and impulses whose threatening reality was only too well known to her. In subsequent weeks she was able to tell, in direct words, how mistreated and helpless she felt, and how she could not share those feelings with a mother she knew to be too fragile to hear them. Although magical thinking still led Jenna to imagine that her play might lead to more real-world neglect, that somehow her mother would know what she'd been playing, she knew she'd never be assaulted or abandoned by the puppets, however badly she treated them.

Children can project feelings onto a puppet or doll that they simply cannot bear owning themselves.

> "And those aren't crocodile tears, either." Eleven-year-old Jermaine heaved with drama as he made my alligator puppet cry.

"What's the matter?" I asked the puppet.

The puppet being too upset to talk, Jermaine explained that the crocodile's grandfather had gotten killed in a boating accident. "Oh," was all I soberly replied as I watched Jermaine comfort the puppet.

"That's okay," he said repeatedly, holding the alligator. "You'll be okay, fella."

Jermaine was a streetwise boy with an attitude. Whatever he felt inside, he wasn't about to show it. "Crying's for babies," he told me later, though he made clear that this alligator was no baby and had good reason to be sad. So did Jermaine, who lost his grandfather in a car crash, a grandfather who was more like a father. By putting it into the puppet alligator, Jermaine changed his grief into a form he could bear and have compassion toward, thus allowing him to begin his mourning, a process that eventually led to more undisguised and heartfelt sadness over his real loss.

But these projected feelings don't have to be exclusively sad.

"Look at that stupid fag!" Thomas sneered. He'd deliberately squeezed a warrior action figure into a checkered dress that he'd grabbed off a small doll. He then topped off the outfit with a wig he'd made out of clay. "You dumb girl fag." Thomas took the tiny play scalpel from a doctor's office set and stuck it between the warrior's legs. "Now we'll cut it off and you'll really be a girl." The transformation complete, Thomas threw the warrior back into the toy bin. "You queer piece of crap."

By providing psychological cover, the doll allowed Thomas to share something quite deep that made him vulnerable to enormous shame. I did not wonder aloud whether it was Thomas, not the warrior, who really wanted to be a girl. My doing so would have ruined everything, short-circuiting the very protective device that the doll play was affording this early adolescent. Though he discarded the she-warrior with utter disdain, disdain meant for himself, he listened with great interest to my empathic statement that life must be very disappointing and frustrating for a warrior who would sometimes rather be a girl.

Children prefer to see their puppets, and not themselves, as frightened, angry, worried, wanting. The puppet, not she, is the greedy one who wants it all. Or it's the puppet, not I, who wants my baby brother dead and gone from my house. By attributing their "bad" thoughts to the puppet, children transfer their internal conflict between good and evil to an arena in which they can battle the badness from without, developmentally, a much easier struggle. Unable to tell of her wish to be naughty, a girl played a noble knight trying to tame a fiery dragon who, depending on her self-regard in the hour, might mercilessly punish or generously forgive and rehabilitate. Somewhat the converse, I have seen a jaded and delinquent teenager turn a shark puppet into the God of the Ocean's helper, expressing in this play a wish to be a good boy, a basic wish he forever disowned in his day-to-day tough-guy existence.

Children also project aspects of themselves that they just plain don't like. "Look at the fat slob," an overweight boy said of my unremarkably average-looking moose puppet. "You're so short I think I'll just step on you," said another about the same puppet, height being that child's issue. My puppets have been seen as stupid, ugly, gross, deformed, unathletic, brainy, smelly, and having the wrong color hair or eyes. Sometimes what a child projects perfectly matches the reality, as when a child with Down's syndrome, a child who was much teased for perpetually farting, tormented a plastic skunk for being so stinky. More frequently, children will see what they have to see regardless of what really is, such as when a girl who disliked her legs found my puppets to be "short and stubby," though of course she knew the puppet, having a hand-hole in its bottom, had no limbs of its own. These harmless but profitable assaults, a spilling over of their own self-criticism, often lead to more compassionate acceptance of the puppets and themselves.

All of these varied self-representative functions can reveal much about the child. More disturbed children who lack an integrated self may employ many different puppets, each holding a limited fragment of their whole self. One autistic boy relied on an epic cast of characters, including the hungry wolf, cuddly lamb, angry moose, and sad duck. When feeling more intact, he would literally embrace all the puppets, feeling at one with them all (Bromfield 1989). More advanced self-growth might be demonstrated as split or dual attributions, depicting good versus evil, needy versus satisfied, dependent versus self-sufficient, male versus female. In such play the puppet on the child's right hand debates the puppet on the left, whereas better integrated children frequently depend on one puppet to contain and express their ranging thoughts and feelings. Doing so aids their confronting and mastering their ambivalence.

As we've all seen, children often use puppets to play out interpersonal conflicts, especially those involving the family. Because the original objects, such as mother and father, are absent from the playroom, the puppets serve as real objects with which complex or painful situations can be staged. Being concrete, puppets permit physical actions and nonverbal expression that speech by itself does not.

> In our first meeting 6-year-old Jerry quickly stuck his wolf puppet into a dollhouse room, using his other hand to squash several other puppets into the same space. Within seconds the police arrested everyone, except for Jerry's own character, the wolf who now lay alone in the house, crying.

This was Jerry's visually telegraphic way of telling an impossible story of how his mother, her boyfriend, and various other lovers and addicts, all of whom frequented their small apartment, were busted by the police, leaving him to live with a relative he hardly knew. Puppets, readily available and easily manipulated, enabled this overwhelmed child to efficiently reveal complicated events more quickly, succinctly, and richly than he could have with words alone, particularly in his first meeting with me. By widening his channel of communication, puppets made possible Jerry's recounting of his complex story without his getting stuck or being prematurely disrupted by the frustration of having too big a tale to tell.

Children's motivations for using puppets to act out interpersonal scenarios vary. Such play, especially if repetitive, may reflect a striving in the service of a developmental task, as when a toddler plays and replays a walrus puppet's migrating and return home. Analogously, children use puppet play to gain mastery over situations in which they've felt, and possibly still feel, helpless, frightened, or out of control. A recent kindergarten graduate orchestrated a puppet entering first grade. Another child, whose parents were divorcing, played a referee puppet futilely determined to make peace between athletes who waged colossal wars following the most trivial fouls.

> Clumsily trying to make a larger lion puppet tie a knot with a string in its mouth, Michael explained that it was securing a smaller lion puppet to the back of a play jeep. Satisfied that the imagined knot was tight—"He's not going anywhere"—the bigger lion nonchalantly climbed into the jeep, then took off at breakneck speed with the baby lion dragging behind screaming for mercy. "Yahoo!" the bigger lion celebrated, delighted by his cub's distress. "Should I go even faster?"

Michael's father, a roofer, would sadistically make his son come along with him on jobs, forcing him to climb tall ladders and sit beside him on steep inclines. On weekends he'd take Michael for frightening joyrides on the back of his motorcycle. Puppets provided Michael, who suffered much abuse from his father, a safe arena in which to avenge his hurt, this play serving as a springboard to our problem-solving ways to protect himself against his father's habitual and sadistic recklessness.

More simply, puppets can help a child enact scenes to show what she has experienced or seen, perhaps to garner sympathy or support, or to convince the therapist that her misdeed was really someone else's fault or that she was unfairly punished by some adult. Puppet play allows children, with relative safety, to tell *their story* replete with wishfulness, muted responsibility, and exaggerated heroism, often necessary and promising precursors to looking at themselves more realistically.

The manipulability of action figures and puppets perfectly suits children's need to turn passive experiences into active ones, reversing their misfortune into good fortune, or at least into re-creating circumstances that are less pained or problematic.

> Sandy tucked two plastic adult figures in the tissue box on the far windowsill. He then came back to line up seven little orange hats on the arm of the chair beside us. "These are how many lives we have." He then set up targets to shoot at, giving us each six missiles to fire. When we played and won—which he ensured we always would—Sandy made the two plastic adult figures pop up and run happily to where we sat.

Of those knowing Sandy's home life, who would not have been able to make sense of his play? He created a videogame, the ultimate of control, in which our well-aimed aggression rewarded us with the return of a plastic man and woman. Sandy's mother was a scientist whose international reputation took her on frequent long and faraway business trips. His father traveled a good deal too, though not as much. "If only I could press a button and make my mom come home just like that," Sandy explained later.

The fact that the child's hand actually sits inside the puppet also bears meaning. Like a facial mask, this hand costume can serve to create a sense of disguise, somewhat disinhibiting the child and fueling the "it's the puppet, not me" spirit of the play. The material limits of the puppet that restrain the hand can enhance the impulse-ridden child's capacity to maintain control while expressing potentially disorganizing material. The good feeling of the puppet's dark, warm interior can invoke regressive and sexual longings, stimulating fantasy play. And though the child holds the puppet on her hand, she may feel that the puppet *holds her*, a miniaturized and concrete embodying of the therapeutic "holding environment" (Winnicott 1945) that, in a small way, helps to foster feelings of psychological security.

Children use puppets in ways other than their intended purpose as play characters. Puppets can be hugged, assaulted, abandoned (and retrieved), used as pillows, and folded up like a pair of socks to become a ball, to name a few possibilities. The fuzziness and softness of puppets can involve masturbatory urgings as well as provide less sexual self-soothing. Through these many and assorted roles, puppets can serve as transitional objects, helping children commute, in an increasingly realistic and mature way, between their inner experience and the world at large (Winnicott 1951).

Although neither necessary nor sufficient for therapeutic change, puppets can serve a helpful cathartic function. For example, the opportunity to shed real and mounting fears can buoy children facing painful and serious medical procedures such as cardiac surgery (Abbott 1990) or bone marrow transplants (Linn 1986). Beyond making the child feel better, emotional relief can lessen stress-related bodily symptoms, delinquent acting out, and other residue of overwhelming tension. A temporary discharge of anxiety can also make the child more accessible to education, reassurance, or problem-solving that in turn can alleviate the source of distress or remedy a life dilemma.

Puppets can also help child patients manage their relationship with us, their therapists.

"Will you feed me?" the Dalmatian puppet asked in a small voice, while its master, a severely learning-disabled seventh-grade girl who was unable to take teachers' help, handed me clay bones to insert in the dog's mouth. "Will you help me learn to do tricks?" it asked me, pushing its back into the palm of my hand. "Can I sleep at your feet?" the dog then asked, making itself a snug bed on my desk.

"Kids *really* play with these things?" Allison asked, seeing we were out of time, gently removing the puppet from her hand. "How queer."

For all of the reasons mentioned above, puppets offered Allison a mode of communicating that allowed for physical activity even when sitting in a chair. The distance created by puppet play permitted her to test our relationship more vigorously. What impulses will we tolerate, and to what intensity? What kind of language or silences are okay? A puppet can ask, perhaps months before a child can, whether it can have snacks, swear, or come as much as it wants.

While serving many of the functions of puppets, action figures are particularly appealing to children, who use them in every imaginable way. They can use them as family in the dollhouse. They can use them for target practice. They can put them into their beds, sit them at the kitchen table, wrap them up in tissue blankets, hide them, find them, throw them, send them sliding down slides into a father's waiting arms, send them down slides into a cauldron of boiling oil, wrap them up in scotchtape straitjackets, or even cram them into the dollhouse play toilet. And they are just the right size to be eaten by my hollow rubber *Tyrannosaurus rex*. Their handy size makes them convenient, rough-and-ready stand-ins when children stage their therapeutic crimes and dramas.

The superhero class of figures lend themselves quite easily to expressing omnipotent fantasies of unlimited powers and strength, particularly for those children who feel unusually weak and helpless bodily, psychologically, or circumstantially. Army men and military-type figures tend to evoke battles involving aggression, pitting good against evil. Civilian setups, such as action figure classrooms and doctor's offices, obviously work well for children playing out conflicts related to those settings.

The dollhouse itself is a useful vehicle for children's play in treatment. Whether portrayed as an impenetrable fortress against intruders and tornadoes or as a home of straw to be easily destroyed by the wolf's first and feeblest huffing, it teaches us much about the child's world. Our child patients can use the dollhouse to construct their homes as they are and as they wish they were (the latter, not uncommonly, resembling the homes we, their therapists, live in). Sometimes children arrange the dollhouse mostly as a test to see what happens next week, to see whether other children mess it up, and whether I let them. Their eventual discovery that I permit every child to use the dollhouse, however grandly set up by the child before, invariably summons issues of their competition for attention and love.

As with any aspect of play or talk therapy, the therapist must be willing to proceed at the child's pace. Even under the pressures of managed care, no patient can proceed faster than he is able to. By this view the therapist intervenes, saying or doing something only when there is something useful to say or do.

When a child's puppet addresses me, I try to respond directly to the puppet, making eye contact with it and talking to it. Children watch closely to see how genuinely we participate in the charade of puppet play. If we interact with the child, ignoring the inquiring or advancing puppet, we risk undoing the original motive for using puppets and discharge the therapeutic impetus. Just as we would not insist that a child play or talk, we do not make demands of the puppet. Rather than order the "barking Snuffy" to speak English, we might note that "Snuffy is barking," and only later and gently invite the puppet dog to share more, in words.

> For many minutes we'd sat in silence, Gary and I making our identical skunk puppets stare into each other's eyes. We intensely watched our characters as if observing a real meeting of living and autonomous creatures.
> "Why's he crying?" the third-grader finally asked.
> "I'm not sure," I answered.
> "He's probably sad about something he can't talk about," Gary explained.

Since his mother had been diagnosed with breast cancer, the once cheery boy had grown sullen, was unable to work at school, and was experiencing severe stomachaches and poor sleep. But he hadn't shed a single tear nor had he been able to share any of his loss with anyone. Allowing our puppets to simply and quietly gaze at one another, I helped fuel Gary's perception of the skunk puppets as "sufficiently alive to give the illusion of a human being with whom one can speak, who will reply and who will actually move" (Rambert 1949, p. 17). This small interaction opened the gates to Gary's improved coping with his mother's illness.

Similarly, the emotional revelations of puppets cannot be hurried. Acceptance of emotions can be conveyed nonverbally, by gently pushing a box of tissues toward a baby frog who cries, for example. When a puppet looks a certain way, but is not described to be feeling a certain way, I am wary of defining the affect prematurely. If a child crunches up a lion's face, we might first note that the "face is all crunched up" rather than "the lion is sad." If we guess wrong, we confound the child's own line of inquiry. Should we guess right, we run the risk of chasing the child away, repeating some parents' tendency to feel and act as if they know best what is in a child's mind. What patients spontaneously offer usually proves more valuable than what we forcibly extract.

As a rule, children are willing to steer their puppet play. Exuberant therapists, especially those who pride themselves on their playfulness and access to fantasy, may be prone to overpowering the child, influencing the play's direction according to their own biases and needs. Contrary to what one might expect, a child typically does not mind being asked, "What should my alligator say [or do] now?" This query urges our child patients to lead the way, opening our window into their psyches, and actually making our job as therapists easier.

Over succeeding sessions, we watch for continuity, but allow for change. When a child wishes to name the puppets, preserving their names and qualities, our recall of that is much appreciated and conveys deep caring. However, that child may one day wish to start anew, making fresh characters with previously unheard-of names. Should we run to show that child that his earlier play was remembered, we may inadvertently retard the natural evolution of play. In such a situation we might ask, "Do you wish to use new names?" or "Is the cow's name still going to be Mr. Bull?"

Children often grow quite invested in and attached to the puppets, using them to express deep and personal feelings. When a child removes her hand from a puppet, her caring may continue. I take care not to mistreat a puppet in the child's presence, for example, tossing it across the room into a toy box only moments after that same puppet has expressed heartfelt grief. The child, however, holds the right to mistreat the puppet that just seconds ago was his dearest confidant. That is the patient's prerogative.

All aspects of puppet play, including form and manifest and latent content, are fair game for observing and examining. In every instance we work together with the child to decipher the meaning and motivation of the play, keeping in mind that puppets and their acts often carry multiple meanings and motives. For example, a sadistic father puppet may reflect qualities of a toxic real parent as well as the child's own hostility. Wild analysis of puppet play, as of any other words or deeds, is of little value and can cause harm. By the therapist's showing the puppet acceptance, admiration, empathy, and judiciously reasoned interventions, the child comes to feel the same in kind.

While many children take to the puppets immediately, others can be pushed toward them, as a form of limit setting, when perhaps their sexual or aggressive play is becoming too intense or dangerous.

Keith, a first-grader who'd been molested by a camp counselor, could not talk of the incident. However, in his third hour he became more vocal. "Kiss my belly," he said, lifting his T-shirt. "Feed me a banana in my butt. Do it. Do it!" As his voice grew louder, he also came closer, abruptly trying to stick his hand under my shirt.

"Here you go," I said, standing up and handing over a puppet. "It's not okay to go into my clothes, but you can do whatever you wish with this guy." Keith eagerly took the puppet he designated to be me.

By suggesting that Keith use a puppet, while making clear that his provocative behavior could not be targeted directly at me, I helped him continue his play associations. This limit redirected his affect and deeds into symbolic play, enabled me to sustain an accepting and empathic posture, ensured our mutual safety, and strengthened his ego controls (Ginott 1959). After all, I was not about to let Keith kill, maim, cook, eat, or rape me; but he could—and with great therapeutic benefit did—do those things, and more, to my puppet namesake.

By allowing a greater and safer opportunity for action of all kinds, puppet play helps children preserve their therapeutic themes and momentum. For similar reasons the puppets make wonderful companions to the doctor's kit, for so much of what my child physicians want to do to me is not allowable (e.g., where they want their needle ultimately to go).

The special role that puppets play in child therapy derives mostly from their facilitating value, their expansion of the communicative repertoire between child and therapist. Puppet play, through its many functions, both invites and enhances the intimacy, disclosure, and self-discovery essential to relationship-based therapies.

The material in this chapter was derived, in part, from "The Use of Puppets in Play Therapy" by R. Bromfield, in *Child and Adolescent Social Work Journal* 12(6): 435–444, copyright © 1995, and used by permission of Plenum Press.

7

SHOOT, TOPPLE, AND ROLL: USING GAMES, BUILDING TOYS, AND GUNS

While puppets and dolls most visibly seem to personify what children think and feel, they can use other play materials to show themselves and to manage being with us. How do children employ games, building toys, and play weapons in their therapies, and how can we maximize their self-clarifying functions?

GAMES

The love of games that the majority of children know does not wait outside the therapy office. "Great! You have Life." ". . . Chutes and Ladders." ". . . Uno." Just seeing their favorites on our shelves puts their minds a little more to rest as they reckon with their having to be in a room with this stranger doing whatever strange business we do. That we have such games tells them, so they assume, that we must like children and like games, or at least understand and respect what *they like*. More important, the games' presence suggests that we will be playing games, that implied structure subduing some of the child's anxiety about how this apparently open-ended and free-flowing hour will be spent. But what do we actually do with games once the therapy is on its way, and how do they help to propel our child patients' exploration?

The most obvious function of games is also the simplest. Games can make children feel comfortable. The material substance of the game, the playing board or card piles, defines an occupied space that helps to organize the child's physical relationship with the therapist. I sit here, you sit there, and neither of us moves any closer. To varying degrees the structure of the game tells the child what to do: he needs to pick a card, read it, and move the game piece as the card dictates. The mechanics of the game—throwing the dice, spinning the pointer—demand attention, limiting how much a child and therapist can talk about personal matters. The overriding play of the game—my turn, your turn—repeatedly and dependably enables the child (and the child's therapeutic load) to be saved by the bell. Holding the cards or counting out the play money gives children something to do with their hands, helping to bind their anxiety.

Playing a game can draw out a child in all of these ways. In the absence of a push or demand to talk, a child may suddenly feel an urge. "My teacher's such a jerk," spoken incidentally while slamming down a winning gin rummy hand, can be the beginning of a constructive discussion of school-related issues. Insulated by the board, distracted by the playing, interrupted by turn-taking, and expected to make eye contact with the game, not us, children can find themselves feeling more relaxed and secure. Much like the kibitzing-inducing powers of bridge or poker, the pleasures and camaraderie of playing games with us can lead children to surrender their guard and begin to reveal themselves.

But we must play our own therapeutic cards carefully. Should we blow a whistle, jump up and down, suddenly stop playing, or show too much attention to our child patients' toes-in-the-water revelations, we will send them, like so many startled hermit crabs, scurrying back to their shells. Thus some turns later, I reply, "Your teacher's a real jerk?" my delayed response implying no urgency, my eyes on the game, not him, maintaining the child's casual posture.

We must be wary of relying too much on the facilitating value of games. Some children, particularly those uncomfortable with the notion of sitting with a therapist, want to play games a lot, if not all the time. For these children board games such as Diplomacy, Risk, and chess reign supreme: by their figuring, the bigger the game (meaning more time-consuming and more complicated), the smaller the burden of talking and being with us. Although these children may protest that they can play a game and talk, often they do little more than hide behind their pawns and knights.

For this reason more intensive board games might best be tucked away for special circumstances, as when working with a child who truly cannot tolerate therapy otherwise. To unnecessarily introduce therapy with these kinds of games can unintentionally trap the therapy, fostering the child's dependency on such a structured crutch, denying her the hour-by-hour experience of getting used to the talking and playing of therapy. In addition, therapists are prone to run to the games with patients to whom we feel unable to connect or with whom we feel otherwise lost as to what to do for the hour. Like the parents we counsel, we sometimes need to reassess our choices. It's okay, and perhaps necessary, for us to change our minds mid-therapy, to decide and tell a child that we won't be playing Monopoly anymore, further explaining that when we do play it, we just don't seem to get the (therapeutic) work done. Even if the work is going forward, we are obliged to put the game away if we judge that it would go faster and better without the distraction.

For some children the social aspect of playing a game is itself constructive.

Randy loved playing Ladybug, a board game in which snails race a spiraling track to the prized ladybug. When first playing, Randy cared only about his turns, needing to be reminded to give me the dice and a chance. He routinely and unintentionally knocked my snail off the board as he moved his own. Randy might as well have been playing by himself.

But it was a good thing he was playing with a therapist, for his egocentric ways had cost him many friends. Even his mother and father didn't like playing with him. As he played the game over and over with me, we came to understand that much of what he did was no more and no less than his naturally unthinking and clumsy way. He had to work hard not to throw the dice everywhere or to move his snail without disturbing my own. My compassionately helping him to see this allowed Randy to begin making allowances for himself. He came to see that he couldn't help messing up the board sometimes, but he could take the time and effort to set it back up to where it was. Slowly he also came to see what it must be like for me to be constantly overlooked in the game. Without my telling him what to do, and without group child therapy, Randy transferred his insights to become a better game player and playmate outside of treatment.

In a comparable fashion, playing games can help children come to terms with their learning disabilities. Although she enjoyed games and friends, 11-year-old Cheri's cognitive problems made game playing difficult at times. She routinely moved her playing piece the wrong number of spaces or even the wrong way, both to and against her advantage, and unwittingly broke the rules. More times than not she miscounted play money and could not add her points in score-tallying games such as Yahtzee. In short, she loved games but could barely play them. The few she could play with some competency, such as Candy Land, bored her fellow sixth-graders. Cheri's game playing typically ended in her quick and utter frustration, with playing pieces and game board thrown everywhere.

In her work with me we repeatedly observed the little big things that called attention to her weaknesses and led to her self-hatred. "I'm so stupid. My cousin in kindergarten can play games better than me." Our work proceeded space by space, roll by roll, even more slowly than did our snail-playing pieces. Over time and many aborted games Cheri came to see how her learning difficulties impaired her playing. She grew to have compassion for herself for having to work so hard at something that she saw came so easily and pleasurably to other children. Rather than reflexively despise herself for being so stupid, she learned to laugh at herself and her inevitable mistakes. She developed coping strategies, for example, learning to banter comfortably while buying herself more time to ponder or make her move. She became more self-protecting, declining to play games that were too much for her and becoming a better negotiator with friends about what games to play. Being such a game lover, she decided to practice more, trying games on her own at home to prepare to play them out with friends. Most of all, she came to better accept her limitations, not just when playing games, but at school and home, allowing her to make better use of the help that her parents and teachers offered.

Games that demand skills beyond the intellectual can similarly exercise children with issues around their perceptual-motor skills. A child's relative lack of skill at games requiring dexterity, such as ring tossing or dart throwing, can bring up feelings of incompetency and low self-esteem, as well as raise even deeper issues involving, for example, one boy's belief that his father, an athlete, loved him less for not being one. This type of game can also help to inform us about how accurately our child patients assess their abilities. Is the child as inept as he moans he is, or, is he actually better coordinated, his self-criticism reflecting unreasonably high standards?

For obvious reasons, game playing provides a forum to deal with conflicts around competition.

An extremely bright child, Joshua would play cribbage keenly and to the death until it appeared that I would lose, at which point he

became a bumbling and inept rival. Afraid of winning, but not
wanting to lose either, Joshua most liked hard-fought ties, those
circumstances in which he could play tough without suffering the
guilt of victory. When unable to avoid winning, Joshua would make
endless excuses on my behalf, dismissing his triumph as lucky and
meaningless. My noting his having won fairly and deservedly led
to his solicitous appeals out of worry that I might be angry and
resentful of having been shown up.

Joshua's oedipal conflicts—meaning in this case his fear that
beating his father would result in loss of his love—led to his profound underachieving, not only in games but in most areas of his
life. As we continually noted his conflicts around our competing,
he came to understand his fear of winning. Real-world progress
accompanied these insights. He became more assertive in expressing his ideas and creativity, and more able to compete intellectually
in situations that allowed it (e.g., spelling bees and debating club).
Joshua engaged in several new activities, such as athletics, which
he'd previously avoided. He also came to have an easier and more
satisfying relationship with his father, whom Joshua had assumed
incorrectly couldn't handle his son's maturing and growing com-
petencies. Above all, he grew capable of feeling the pride and joy
of his many accomplishments and was willing to try things he was
not quite as adept at.

Perhaps most common to our offices are the narcissistically
vulnerable children for whom losing a game is a dreaded injury to
be avoided at all costs.

"Come on, you bastard. Deal the cards. What a piece of crap you
are. You can't even shuffle cards good," Fritz accused.
  These tirades were no surprise. When I won at pick-up sticks,
he accused me of cheating. I'd also, so he judged, tricked him at
Chinese checkers. The sorest of losers, Fritz was not even a pleasant
winner. "Loser. You're such a pathetic loser. I can't believe how
stupid you are."

Only by our struggling around each and every game, by examining Fritz's need to put me down mercilessly, did he grow stronger and more able to withstand the outcome of the game, whether or not it was in his favor.

"Why, when you win, do I have to be a complete fool?" "Why, when I win, do you need to believe that I won by dishonesty?" "Why can't we both try hard at a game in which only one person can win? And for that matter," we came to ask together, "why can't one of us win without either of us being worthless or sleazy?"

Rather than trying to teach Fritz to play fair, I provided a safe opportunity in which he might admit to himself just how badly he had to win. Rather than criticizing his ruthless game-playing ways, I respectfully honored his need to protect an utterly fragile self-image, an image that losing a little game of checkers could send reeling. By the time Fritz could state out loud (and with a smile), "I must win every game!" he had become quite tolerant of losing, and sometimes even intentionally misplayed so that I might win. The progress he made with our game playing also served as a springboard from which he approached his bigger and broader susceptibility to injury from the world in his daily life.

Playing with children like Fritz forces us to confront the question of cheating. With Fritz, for whom winning seemed to mean surviving, I chose not to confront or limit his cheating. To do so would have put him on the defensive and neglected the all-important protective function it served. As he became more aware of that need, he himself began to note—with laughter and delight—how sneaky he could be. Gradually he gave up his cheating, his playing pieces now demonstrably revealing his sentiments by teasing my piece, knocking it down, and literally running rings around it, bringing his once deceitful cheating into the therapeutic realm for examination. However, as with most matters of therapy, there are no golden rules we can rely on when a child cheats.

We can usually assume that children who cheat for our benefit as well as their own—smiling while sneaking their man ahead, delib-

erately counting themselves extra play money even as we watch—
are already conflicted. That they flaunt their cheating in our face
suggests they are acting out something interpersonal, wanting our
attention, our reaction, our limits. In these instances, noting their
amusement and following where it leads will suffice in successful
exploration of what it means, leading to the child's giving up that
behavior. Often we may find that children who cheat in this way are
telling us that they feel one down or in some way impotent in their
world and need to wield some power to their advantage.

But when we work with more singularly sociopathic children, those lacking conscience or those who are teetering pre-
cariously on the fence between a decent life and delinquency, we
may not wish to humor their cheating, especially when it is intended to manipulate us and the game without our knowing. "You
moved your man an extra space," I do not hesitate to point out,
while also wondering out loud why he needs to cheat. "Cheat
much?" I'll ask, listening carefully to the bragging list of ways in
which the child beats the system and his playmates. While our
discussion and game playing may help, it is a steady combination
of empathy and limits, with heavy behavioral intervention in his
school and home life, that promise the most hope and help to the
seriously wayward child.

The game playing itself can carry a symbolic meaning for the
child. One high school senior, anticipating going off to college,
found herself drawn to Candy Land, which evoked intense memories of a childhood and home she was unsure about leaving. Its
opposite is the over-coddled first-grader who brought a chess set
to his session, proclaiming that my games were for babies. Young
children use through–the–forest–type board games to play out fears
of a dangerous world and of growing up. Games such as Sorry and
Chutes and Ladders give our patients a wonderful opportunity to
safely express their aggression as they send us back to Go or watch
with glee as we slide backwards to square one.

The framework of the games we play also tends to bring up
much for the child. The child's view of questions concerning who

goes first, who's the banker, what constitutes winning, and who, winner or loser, starts the next game become relevant fodder for examining. And what do we do when the hour ends but the game is ongoing? Stopping on time with a child who is winning can be difficult but more clinically useful than promising to preserve the game for the following session.

BUILDING TOYS

My large cardboard blocks are the most used toys in my office. I suspect their popularity is attributable to their value in so many varying kinds of play. Being large and easy to hold, blocks make a rough-and-ready toy that especially suits younger children and those with motor difficulties.

Blocks offer the child an easy way to be with us in the beginning, a way that allows for physical movement and fairly certain success. Many children initially use them to build towers, seeing how high they can go, taking great pleasure when their blocks pass my head, some reaching to the ceiling. These early constructions, I've found, often move the child to ask that we invite their mother or father in from the waiting room to show off their creations.

In a simple and concrete way blocks enable the child to work on a problem, such as making a tower that won't tumble. Through repeated trial and error children can experiment their way to a stronger and taller structure, each bit of success enhancing their confidence and giving them a greater sense of influence over their environment and world. It is impressive, indeed, to observe children push themselves to higher standards and more complex designs as they progress, making clear that it is the process, not some static result, that motivates their efforts.

Children often use blocks to facilitate their fantasy play with other toys, building zoos for their animals, garages for their cars, and homes for the puppets. One 12-year-old used such a setup to resolve his dislike for a new stepfather.

"We only have a couple of minutes left," I announced. "Just one more thing," Devon replied as he put the finishing touches on an elaborate army base he'd made out of blocks. The base's invincibility apparently being uncertain, Devon had placed a green army man, gun, or tank in every nook and cranny of his construction. "There," Devon said, placing one lone soldier in front of and facing his formidable force. "That's your army." Devon spent the last seconds demolishing my minute battalion.

Devon replicated this play every week for months, each hour giving me a few more men, then some guns, then tanks. Although he never once mentioned the stepfather whom—I knew from his parents—he resented for having stolen his mother and for trying to enforce rules like a real father, his relationship with the man steadily grew better through this period. By the time our forces had become equally proportioned, Devon was able to describe how small and overpowered he felt by his parents' divorce and his mother's remarriage. By maintaining the security of his sturdy block base, Devon was able to relinquish and share more of the power with me and his stepfather.

Children soon realize that the same blocks that can be used with puppets and action figures can be used to build things big enough to accommodate their own bodies.

Eight-year-old Coby was an impulsive and anxious boy who could not sit still. The fact that he'd recently suffered a first epileptic seizure only raised his fear of losing control to an even higher level. For months Coby lay on the floor while I built block fences around him, fences that he'd suddenly break through with kicking and thrashing. Each week he asked that the bordering blocks be brought closer to him, requiring that he lie increasingly motionless so as not to disrupt them.

By controlling his body to be perfectly still, then cataclysmi-cally wild, Coby began to master his self-control as well as the overwhelming dread of another seizure. This mastery also brought increased coping with his illness, a willingness to learn techniques to relax, more cooperation with his medicine, and more constructive expression of the rage he felt over having epilepsy.

Children frequently build block fortresses and walls to hide behind, protect themselves, and shut us out. "My mother can make me come here, but she can't make me talk to you," one ambivalent child called to me from inside the cave he'd built himself. He was right, too. The shelter of his cave, however, allowed him to engage with me around his misgiving about therapy, a connection that soon brought a strong attachment to me and treatment.

One boy, sitting on the throne he'd made, ruled as king that his separated parents would reunite. Two children tried to resolve their fear of death: one child created a live-forever box while the second went to sleep in the coffin she'd made herself. "Woof. Woof. Pat me," barked one teenager from inside her block doghouse, this play revealing the truth behind her tough, don't-need-nobody exterior. And more than one younger child has dealt with his worries about growing up by laying a block path on which he must stay lest he fall into quicksand, deep waters, and alligator-infested swamps. Children build themselves high chairs, cribs, corrals, cages, and castles. The ways our child patients use the blocks in relation to themselves are endless.

Being big, noisy (when they fall), harmless, and rather indestructible (they can support a grown man's weight), the cardboard blocks also admirably serve to express aggression.

A shy boy, Craig gave the term *inhibited* new meaning. He spoke in almost a whisper and moved as if wrapped in a mummy suit. He seldom asked for anything and complained of little. His passivity frustrated his family, teachers, and friends beyond belief. His seemingly quiet and selfless posture somehow made more noise and called more attention to himself than were he able to speak his mind.

In his therapy Craig built small and solid towers that, though they reached only to my waist, he worried might fall on and kill me. Gingerly, he would tap them, each time diving to the ground to withstand the earthshaking avalanche his projected rage caused him to anticipate. Gradually he built much higher towers that he knocked down with venom.

Just as gradually Craig came to talk and laugh more loudly, move more robustly, protest, and just plain feel stronger and better. The blocks provided a lively and safe forum in which to begin experimenting with the intense anger and frustration that he held so tightly inside himself. Of no surprise, the people in Craig's life found his noisy and complaining self much easier and more enjoyable to be with, a self that soon quieted, not out of fear, but out of genuine contentment and greater confidence.

More reckless children can exercise their self-control by toppling towers that we build or by ruining only parts of a structure, for example, or by having to describe their aggressive intent verbally before acting on it. Blocks make good targets for punching, kung fu'ing and—a favorite of the children—pretend blowing up. Block houses can be kicked apart, huffed and puffed down by a demonic wolf, and destroyed by acts of war and Mother Nature.

Children also enjoy construction toys such as Lincoln Logs, Tinker Toys, and Erector Sets. Children use my plastic Erector Set–like toy to make various contraptions to accompany their play: cranes to lift broken cars, cranes to lift and torture vicious dinosaurs, magic swords, a vault to hide their money, and surgical instruments to transform their gender. I tend to avoid Lego-type toys for I've found their all-consumingness to obstruct the child's play, and the children who love them tend to be children who have them at home.

Early in my practice I discovered that the box of dominoes on my desk, rarely used to play the game proper, were constantly being used to build domino knockdowns. Soon after, I put several more boxes into a straw basket that is a veritable staple of my play materials. Children can construct these intricate designs while talking. This play is the ultimate activity for children who are prone to overwhelming frustration, for these knockdowns often fall from the slightest misstep or shaken desk.

For similar reasons I have wooden blocks from the recycling shop of Boston's Children's Museum instead of a set of regular ones. My blocks are all different sizes, no two alike. Children who may find the asymmetry originally annoying soon find them interesting and a challenge that further promotes their growing easier with frustration, imbalance, and the imperfection of life. These blocks also give children with shaky esteem ample opportunity to good-naturedly belittle my toys and the therapy as second-hand and defective, making for good lead-ins to their looking at why they need to see themselves in such a critical light.

GUNS

On top of old Smokey,
    all covered with blood,
I shot my poor teacher,
    with a 40-foot gun.
I went to her funeral,
    I went to her grave,
Instead of flowers,
    I brought a grenade.
But in the morning,
    she wasn't quite dead,
So I took a bazooka,
    and blew off her head.

Appalled? What kind of child would say, no less think, such a thing? A vicious hooligan, probably, perhaps one who's already done his share of fighting and violence. A deranged product of society? The offspring of an absent father? Maybe this child was abused. What else could account for such sick and malevolent feeling?

Actually, this was told to me by a sweet, kind, honest, hardworking young girl who wouldn't have hurt a fly if her life depended on it. She was a helpful daughter and a devoted grandchild and took reliable care of the family pets. She came to therapy because she worried too much. She worried that she and those she loved might die. She worried that everything might go wrong. And most of all, she worried that her human less-than-saintly thoughts meant she was a bad girl who deserved to be severely punished. (Incidentally, like everyone else, our young poet's teacher liked her very much and thought her a jewel in her class.)

I introduce this discussion of guns somewhat provocatively for the topic has understandably grown quite controversial over the past years. Toy guns, once every boy's right, have been banished by many. I recall reading an ad by a major stuffed-animal manufacturer that asked, "Is it any wonder that our prisons are full?" above pictures of a green grenade, a blue plane, a red-and-white-striped rocket, a camouflaged army tank, and a water pistol.

If raising a healthy and decent human being only *could* be accomplished by purchasing the right toy! Can a small, plastic water gun truly obliterate the positive influence of a loving, respectful, and consistent upbringing? And what feeble power can a fleecy lamb wield in the face of a neglecting and abusive home? I've worked with violent children who since birth had owned stuffed animals— nice ones, too. Some of them had tortured these toys with real hammers, knives, and picks as toddlers before they'd ever laid their hands or eyes on a play weapon. Each and every one of these children came from horrible circumstances.

Whether or not we like to see or feel its presence, aggression is everywhere, throughout the world, at home, and within each of us. Our job as therapists is to help children grow into comfortably nonviolent adults who can solve their needs and problems constructively. How can children come to terms with something considered alien, nonexistent, or worthy of permanent exorcism (as if that were possible)? Both ignoring and freely expressing one's aggression represent easy ways out. Struggling to better understand and manage it is a much harder task, but well worth the effort in its benefit to each of us individually and as a society.

Is it any surprise that many of the parents who've criticized my having toy guns have had children whose anger has been wholly out of control? Consider Tucker.

When Tucker's parents came to me, his public first-grade classroom was feeling unable to keep him there. A big child, he was forever bullying other children, especially those younger and smaller than he. If he felt sufficiently slighted or unattended to—which didn't take much—he'd strike out, often viciously, kicking a child even after there'd been a surrender and supposed treaty. But the main reason his parents had brought him to me was his thwarted attempt to push his baby brother's carriage off a ledge.

Though the majority of children who come to me with heady reputations prove to be rather meek and pliable in the therapy hour, Tucker treated me no better than the others in his life. He tried to break toys, constantly put me down, and bragged of the violent things he'd do to all who got in his way. In his play Tucker frenetically created "Crazy Town," a place where everyone was vulnerable to abuse and mistreatment.

In our first month together we began to see progress. Tucker broke less and ranted more. He cried several times about how crazy he gets. He even said, explicitly, that he wanted help. However, his parents, seeing that I had toy guns in my office, became quite critical and challenging of me. Although I empathized with their philosophy about guns in our society, I tried my best to explain how my Nerf blaster—a long plastic orange tube with a bright yellow push plunger—was a healthy, harmless toy that looked nothing at all like a real gun. I could have lived without that toy if it would have eased their minds, but Tucker's parents asked that I not allow their son to even play out aggression in his therapy. My best attempts to convey understanding failed and these parents pulled their child out of treatment.

Though there was clearly more to their agenda, Tucker's parents expressed an increasingly common attitude toward play guns: that they are bad, that they confuse children, that they foster violence and violent solutions to life's problems, and that they negate goodness, caring, and love. I can grasp that attitude unquestionably. But the truth, at least in therapy, is different.

Play guns are first and foremost, if not exclusively, a way to express hostility. It's that simple. I have never seen a child use a gun to talk, to eat food with, to write with, or to make a sheltering home out of. Almost always children use the gun to shoot; occasionally, if frustrated by their inaccuracy, they use the gun to whack down their targets. But if aggression is such a part of the human experience, and its control is so critical yet perilous, aren't toys that advance its mastery to be applauded?

> Lev had a fierce temper and was prone to letting his anger out on whoever was handy, a playmate, a sibling, a parent, or even a teacher. On the flip side, however, when not irate, he tended to be a timid and withdrawn child, apt to be bullied himself until pushed to his limits. Like Tucker's mother, Lev's mother was adamantly opposed to toy weapons. Even after Lev showed me his anger by kicking a heating baseboard off the wall, she feared that playing with my toy gun might make him gun-happy and more comfortable with violence. Upon seeing my toy gun, she was aghast and openly confessed her confusion. She wanted him to get my help but was upset by what she saw.

Unlike Tucker's mother, Lev's mother could see a distinction between her attitude in general and her son's therapeutic needs. She also was aware that her opinion might reflect her own issues around aggression. Over the course of her son's useful treatment, she came to see how her worldview derived from her having lived with an abusive father and her seeing men, even her beloved son, as inherently evil. While helping her to understand her son's anger as well as her own, our good work together did not erode her broader values and battle against guns, nuclear power, and war in general. In fact, in the course of growing much more comfortable with her son's play, even with toy guns, she found the truer source of her conflicts and channeled her public efforts toward supporting a shelter for women who'd been abused.

Ironically, it is often the children who exhibit intense and dangerous outbursts in their lives who are most wary of playing with my toy guns. They shoot hesitantly and quickly toss the gun down, so fearful are they that their hostile impulses will get out of hand. These children especially benefit from play with the gun, learning to shoot more vigorously without losing all control and without shooting at my face or my glass-enclosed pictures.

Just as games can loosen children's self-revelations, shooting can tap children's anger, the safeness of this expression often leading them to talk more freely about what is bothering them and what is making them so enraged.

> Kenny presented as the most generous and caring young man. An eighth-grader, he did well in school and was a good friend and son. However, he suffered intense jealousy of a younger sister that drove him to treat her miserably, often bordering on the abusive.
>
> When asked about her, Kenny nearly always denied any feeling, claiming that she was a good sister whom he appreciated. It was only after weeks of his staging a shooting gallery at bear figures that he, unable to hit the little girl bear, began a tirade about his resentment over little girls. A creature of habit, Kenny spent each of his succeeding hours shooting at this little figure. As he spoke more and more openly of his envy of his sister and his fear that she was loved more, he made room for the guilt-ridden and loving feelings he'd long ago lost touch with.

Feelings of insignificance, injury, neglect, and powerlessness often fuel the abuse and violence that pervade modern life; it's no different with many of the children we treat. Thus, when children come to us ready for a good fight, we try to keep in mind the inner hurt and sense of smallness that likely propels their need to flaunt a big gun. "Wow, you are so big and powerful," I'll first comment to a child who proudly wags the big gun between his legs, before I'll try to explore what experiences are making him feel so little. "With a weapon like that no one can hurt you," I'll note with admiration to a child who sits behind his block fortress, his gun vigilantly aimed outward.

If a play gun is to help a child manage his aggression, limits are of course critical. I don't allow shooting guns to be pointed at me or at anything breakable. Routinely I take away the gun as soon as the child breaks that rule, even just shooting me in the foot. I offer them large action figures as my surrogates, figures they can shoot to their heart's content. While I seldom interfere with the child–parent relationship—meaning I do not jump in to set limits that the parent cannot—I do not allow the child to shoot at his family or siblings. If he does, I take quick and certain responsibility for removing the gun from the child's hands. To allow him to break something or hurt somebody is destructive and countertherapeutic. With this structure the vast majority of children promptly learn how to use the toy gun responsibly and for their therapeutic welfare.

In addition to just shooting, children often incorporate smaller play guns into their fantasy play. Children, I find, are most drawn to spy and police kits that allow them to be the good guys, notoriously fighting aggression with aggression, fire with fire, killing the bad guys before they kill us. Children also like to experiment with being the bad guys who must be tamed and shown the ways of proper civilization.

Needless to say, with gun play and almost any other play in the office, we must assess what is happening in the context of what we know about today's hour, current stresses, the child's broader circumstances, personality functioning, and the social environment in which he lives. Would we spend hours staging gunfights with a child who'd actually shot and killed someone? No. But then the kind of child for whom gun play is wrong is probably a child who needs treatment much more intensive and behavioral than the kind of traditional play therapy described here.

8

DRAWING OUT
THE CHILD:
ARTWORK
IN THERAPY

In their efforts to connect, communicate, and cope with us and their therapies, children use whatever means and resources they possess or can find. They play. They talk. And they draw. They draw little pictures and big ones. Sophisticated and primitive. Well done and much less well done. Whatever the nature of the drawing, it serves as one major conduit between the child and the therapist. This chapter examines the many functions and nuances that characterize children's art in therapy.

When first meeting our child patients, many of us offer them the opportunity to draw. We do so not only to collect what can be a rich harvest of data, but also to help put them at ease. Just as we adults typically find it easier to meet a stranger while smoking, or holding a golf club, or pushing our child through the supermarket, many children feel more comfortable with us while holding a crayon. Drawing can help break the ice, providing a safe activity for child and therapist to begin getting to know one another.

We help to facilitate that goal by making our invitations to draw inviting, meaning void of demand or expectation. Should we show too much enthusiasm for drawing, we risk chasing the child away or trapping the child who doesn't like to draw. "Would you like to draw? There are markers and paper should you wish at any time." Phrasing our offer in these terms gives children the space to decline without feeling they have somehow failed or defied us so early in the relationship.

Children who want to draw may ask what they should draw. Our suggesting that perhaps they might know what they'd like to draw is routine enough, their asking us having represented more of a bow to our authority than any indecision on their part. Although whatever they draw will likely reveal much about themselves, what they first decide to draw will more generally reflect their wish to wow us with their ability. That is, children will often choose to draw not what will most communicate their psychological circumstances and suffering, but the picture they can draw best. If it's a mean sunflower, we can bet we'll get sunflowers. Should sneakers with untied laces be their forte, it's sneakers we'll get.

When a girl asks us explicitly or looks to us for guidance, we don't succumb immediately. "It's not easy to decide, is it?" "What pictures are you thinking about?" "What would you like me to suggest?" Such casual remarks may open up some meaningful discussion about this child's difficulty deciding for herself and perhaps about her broader difficulties in life. We may find that she has dozens of good ideas but feels uncertain about asserting them for fear of displeasing me. Or she may tell us that her mind is blank and that this is a problem for her when teachers ask her to write stories or when friends want to play in fantasy. Once clear that the child needs our help, we may suggest several items (e.g., a child, a family, a tree, some place or thing you like). Intriguingly, it is only after we've made suggestions that some reticent children suddenly come up with their own and better ideas about what to draw.

Whatever she ultimately draws, and whenever in the therapy she draws it, the child's creations and creating will likely tell us much about herself. Before her crayon even touches the paper we can begin to glean information about her. How does she prepare her work space? Does she grab a million sheets of paper while dumping the entire bucket of markers, tossing the top of the marker she's about to use onto the floor? Or does she tease a single sheet of paper off the heap, lining it up just the way she wants before beginning? One child draws with the first utensil she finds; another spends minutes trying out markers until she finds the right color with the right point. Does the child move at the speed of light or more like a turtle who plans its way? Does she draw tentatively, her pencil etching barely visible, or does she wield the marker like a carving knife? Is her picture comfortably sparse like a Shaker home, or is it overflowing with too much, the child compulsively filling in every last empty space? These observations begin to inform us about the girl's intellect, neurological abnormalities, self-discipline, work style, and, certainly, how she may approach tasks at school, particularly those involving drawing or, perhaps, written work.

How children manage their errors or changes of mind can further describe themselves.

> Gary angrily crumpled up his paper and threw it onto the pile that had been accumulating for the past fifteen minutes. Wanting to draw me a picture of his new bicycle, Gary had made no less than two dozen attempts. As soon as the front wheel, which he drew hastily, did not appear perfectly round, Gary disgustedly crossed out what he'd drawn and began anew. Although only the first hour, such frustrating experience prophesied Gary's year-long treatment as centering around harsh self-criticism and how readily he gave up on himself.

Every stroke less than perfect sent Gary's esteem spiraling downward. Other children, no less perfectionistic, however, are not as narcissistically vulnerable. Over and over these children sketch, then erase, sketch, then erase. Although, like Gary, they are ever disappointed with what they do, they have the capacity not only to scrutinize their work, but to fix it until it meets their high standards. Others do their correcting by simply coloring over their mistakes with bolder and bigger markers, proudly handing over drawings that are a mess. Still others recognize that their drawing is not at all what they wished, know that they lack the skill or interest in doing more, surrender their marker, and make clear that they'd rather talk or play.

Perhaps the first thing we notice about a child's drawing is the skill employed. Some children, unsurprisingly, are much more artistic than others. Although children's drawings can reveal something about their intellect (and there are scoring systems for extrapolating IQ from a child's drawing of a person), one needs to exercise caution. A child who is unmotivated, who dislikes drawing, or who is highly intelligent but motorically delayed can display remarkably poor artwork, suggestive of low intelligence. More definite assumptions about cognition and intellect are probably better found in the ongoing language and behavior or the therapeutic relationship, or better yet from standardized psychological and educational testing.

As is true of many other human endeavors, children who draw better generally tend to like drawing more. However, this is not a firm enough principle to rely on in our work. Once children who draw poorly or hastily come to recognize the communicative powers that drawing can hold, they often turn to it as a significant facet of their therapy. When they feel we've noted their skills, even the accomplished artists are wont to pursue their artwork much in the spirit of Pictionary, drawing only as much and for how long as it takes to get their message across to us. However much of an advantage artistic talents can lend, fine or complex drawings are no more likely to carry or communicate more meaning than are their simpler and more primitive counterparts.

Almost any drawn object or thing can tell us so much about our patients, but their drawings of a child represent the mother lode. No other subject matter so vigorously pulls for children's perception of themselves. One bully's drawing of himself as bigger than a house suggested his narcissistic and counterphobic need not to see himself as the small child he was. A second, equally small boy who lived in an overwhelmingly chaotic home out of his control drew a boy the size of the dandelions, portraying the impotence he felt. A child with a muscular problem drew a girl with puny arms as did a boy who feared beating up the sister over whom he felt so jealous.

Just as we do with the real children who enter our office, we look at how these drawn children are dressed. Are they wearing appropriate clothes for their age, the setting, and the weather? Do they wear clothes whose colorfulness contrasts with their own dark apparel and mood? Or is there a figure dressed in black, as if mourning? Does that boy have a tattoo that says "Mom" on his arm, and is that girl wearing a sexy evening gown to school? Relatedly, do these children in the pictures appear their age, well cared for, happy? Children who are drawn nude or with invisible clothes are of particular concern, as they tend to speak to issues of reality testing, abuse, and perceptions of exquisite exposure and shame (though, of course, not necessarily).

The affect displayed, incidentally, may not seem to directly reflect what the child feels. A happy-go-lucky girl standing amid butterflies may tell us about a happy-go-lucky girl who loves nature; a sad girl who would like to be a happy-go-lucky girl who is at home with nature; or—and by no means the only alternative explanation—an abused and angry girl who, resentful that she was robbed of her happy-go-lucky butterfly of a childhood, feels too afraid or mistrustful to share it.

The portrayed child often exhibits unmistakable qualities that tell of its creator. One boy, who I later learned wanted dearly to be a girl, drew a boy wearing a ruffled and flowing skirt. An adorable and petite adolescent girl, feeling the onslaught of puberty, drew herself as a bloated young woman embarrassed by her burgeoning sexuality (see Drawing 8-1). A raging girl whose neglecting mother demanded her politeness drew a shark whose teeth were covered with a mask.

Drawing 8–1

140

Needless to say the content and setting enhance the meaning to be found in drawings. A child about to be guillotined paints a picture different from that of the child atop the Olympic gold medal pedestal. Seeing a child aboard a colorful Noah's ark worries us less than seeing that same child alone in a dilapidated lifeboat adrift on a stormy sea. Seeing a scene in which a child takes positive, self-protective action (e.g., slays a fiery dragon) similarly encourages us more than the child who helplessly screams from the attic window of a burning house.

Some children prefer drawing an animal rather than a child. Despite the species barrier, the self-revelations here can be just as relevant. One third-grader, referred for poor self-esteem secondary to a learning disorder, drew a dinosaur that was "too stupid to add one plus one" (see Drawing 8-2). Some weeks into treatment a depressed boy, unable or unwilling to talk with anyone, including me, drew a possum who, the child told me, wished it could just crawl back into its mother's pouch, evoking significant discussion of his understandable reaction to having been raised by a depressed and unavailable mother (see Drawing 8-3). Thus, it makes sense that we also see lots of cuddly bunnies, puppies, and other baby animals, representations of many a child's longing for love and nurturing.

The setting and atmosphere of a drawing also make us wonder. Why is that suicidal girl drawing us pictures of a sun drenched farm? Because that's where she wants to live? Because she thinks that's what we want? Because she's not sure she can show us what she really feels? Or, as it turned out, because she wanted to make the point of just how deceptively wonderful the relative's home where she was abused appeared to the world. Do the houses look inviting, scary, decrepit? Fire shooting from the windows means something very different from smoke curling up from the chimney.

One need not be a psychologist to know that dark skies often signal gloom and doom, as do clouds and rain often signify tears and sadness. Cold and dark often accompany loneliness, unless of course

Drawing 8–2

Drawing 8–3

the child is portrayed snuggled cozily and happily under a blanket beside a loved parent and in front of a crackling fireplace. Is the child personified as a country or city mouse? What about those natural disasters we see so often and what do they mean? Is that volcano telling us something about an overly self-controlled adolescent's mounting fury or his fear of his father's wrath or, as happens so commonly, is it about both? I've found earthquakes, lightning, floods, and meteor collisions to be a staple of children's drawing.

> Rosalie drew a very nice picture of a very nice day. All seemed well until I asked about the hole in the tree and learned that was where "a baby squirrel was left to starve and rot" over the winter. That awful image, and not the happy sunshine, was what occupied this grossly neglected girl's work with me (see Drawing 8-4).

We know of course that children's drawings often tell us about life at home with the family. We take care to note whom the child's figure stands next to and whom it is isolated from. Why is the child's figure bigger than the shriveled parents (because they aren't present or able to discipline)? We can't help but be curious when one parent is drawn strikingly larger than the other (more beloved, more effective, or maybe more feared and abusive?).

Drawing 8–4

What is the family doing? Partaking in a fun family activity or cooperatively cooking dinner? Or does the picture depict children getting into trouble while a drinking father and crying mother fight in the kitchen? Are characters, especially the child's, firmly distinct from others? The confusing merging of a grown child and mother can be worrisome as can a child's continually redefining and redrawing one family member as another. Just as we observe everything about the children our child patients draw, we look carefully at their portrayals of parents and other significant people in their lives. Although that she-devil mother with horns may reflect neither a bad mother nor a disturbed son, we nonetheless tuck that little piece of data away as we proceed with the child's self-exploration.

In addition to what is in the picture, we might be interested in what isn't.

In the final hour of his successful therapy, Eric drew me a picture of a helicopter hovering about the water (see Drawing 8-5). A ladder hung from the helicopter, and a terrified man dangled just inches from a hungry shark's toothy mouth. It was only after most of the hour that we discovered the secret message in Eric's good-bye card to me. No one was flying the helicopter. Eric, in his poignant drawing, had shown precisely his feeling, his fear that living life without my guidance and support, without me in the cockpit, would be precarious and catastrophic. Fortunately, and to his astonishment alone, he did just fine flying solo.

Similarly, when a child drawn in a picture seems to look askance or off to the side, I may ask, "What is the child looking at?" Intrigued by my strange question and liking the side-handed interest I'm showing, children usually come up with an answer that is worth our time. Should a gun be shooting, "Where, to what target are those bullets aimed, is that bombing being dropped." Babies without parents, houses without windows, anything without what it usually comes with, I question.

Drawing 8-5

As with every communication, we can assume that what children draw for us or in our presence has some meaning in our relationship. Snails burrowed in their shells and bears peering out from their caves make me wonder whether a child is having some doubts about the spotlight of therapy and perhaps of life. When a young girl draws a young girl who asks in a speech balloon, "Am I pretty?" I must wonder if she's asking me. And can a child's vehement request that I rip up and discard a drawing of a boy covered with acne, boils, prickles, quills, and poison not say something about his self-disgust and his disbelief that I could want to do anything but dispose of him from my office and the relationship?

> Eleven-year-old Vicky had been abused for some time earlier in her childhood. Although she had every reason to be enraged and defiant, she was thoroughly compliant and made every effort to please everyone, including me as her therapist. She ceaselessly made me "I love you" cards adorned with chains of hearts and drew pictures full of happy times and happy people. Any observations I made about the compulsiveness of this artwork seemed only to make her anxious, ratcheting the level of her drivenness up a notch. Not until well into her therapy, after she'd grown sufficiently trusting, did she come to understand that she went overboard on the love cards out of fear that I would abuse and hurt her as others had.

Children's drawing functions to express things that are hard to express otherwise.

> Thad, a sixth-grader at a special school, could become floridly psychotic under stress. Unwanted aggressive and sexual thoughts tortured him as did a pervasive sense of himself as massively defective and repugnant. So blinded was he by the cataclysmic flaws he saw in himself (and which he imagined the world saw, too), he had no awareness of his formidable intellect and strengths.
> Prior to our working together, horrifying ideation and impulses often flooded Thad, leading to self-destructive behaviors. As his therapy evolved, however, he came to use drawing as a reliable

and safe means of sharing his inner world, a world that was too complex, primitive, and, he judged, diseased to speak aloud. By using his drawings as containers and springboards for his tumultuous conflicts (e.g., his depiction of a sadistic gender-changing clinic that incorporated oral, anal, and phallic conflicts and ruin), Thad was able to exercise greater self-control, enabling some constructive work in therapy.

Sometimes what the child can't express directly may not be crazy but may be intolerably painful.

Ryan, a first-grader, was confused. He had never known his biological father and he was glad that his mother had finally married. Moreover, he was very fond of his stepfather, a good man who was devoted to both Ryan and his mom. Because of this Ryan did not understand the intense jealousy that had begun literally to eat away at him since the wedding.

It was a drawing that shed light on Ryan's pain (see Drawing 8-6). That palpable caricature of Ryan's oedipal plight—his being locked out of a bedroom in which he fantasized his mother and stepfather had sex—taught us both that what had really gotten Ryan's goat was that he could no longer go in and out of his mother's room as he'd long grown accustomed to doing. This led to broader, useful discussions about the many ways Ryan now had to share his kingdom.

The unspeakable is not always ugly or taboo, either. Sometimes it's the wonderfulness, the wholesome specialness, of what the child thinks or feels that makes it inexpressible through words alone.

Guy, a teenage boy with Down's syndrome, seldom drew. He didn't like to draw as it came very difficult to him. But he came to one session needing to. He worked for most of the hour, painstakingly drawing something that I could not make out.

"There's something you really want me to understand," I said, when he showed me his drawing.

Drawing 8-6

"Yes, I do," Guy crowed, his eyes watering. With my patient query and help he explained his drawing, a blueprint of the home he would like to have as an adult. With great pride and satisfaction he pointed out its quintessential feature. "See, it has wheels," he said, "so my parents can pull it behind their car." This wonderful image was Guy's fantastic and moving solution to his ambivalent wish and fear of growing up and away from his parents.

While a vast majority of children's artworks are oneshot deals meant to facilitate a moment, soon to grow into obsolescence, a child occasionally uses a series of drawing projects as part of an ongoing theme in his therapy.

Leroy, a high-functioning autistic boy, dealt with his transfer from another therapist to me by creating detailed schematics of the old subway line that brought him to therapy and the new line that was replacing it. Each week, for months, Leroy would build one more station that, over many months, was assembled into a subway world that integrated the two lines, the old and the new, allowing for his fantasy of being able to use the new line (and new therapist) without having to wholly give up the old line (and therapist before me). [Bromfield 1997, Chapter 5]

The creative and unpredictable ways in which children use drawings to further their therapies is impressive. One girl, whose sibling envy had reached meteoric proportion, drew before-and-after pictures that showed, more vividly than ten thousand words could have, how her life had come undone by her sister's birth (see Drawings 8-7 and 8-8). No less dramatically did her clever use of a no–babies–allowed–here symbol illustrate her wish that her sister had never been born (see Drawing 8-9). Wanting to convince me of just how nasty and perilous life could be at his home, one boy drew me hazardous mazes from which I could not escape without death or other mishap (see Drawing 8-10).

Before

After

Drawing 8–7

151

Before

After

Drawing 8–8

Drawing 8–9

Start

Finish

The
Maze
of
Many
Pits

One Way

Drawing 8–10

How could words have expressed the preoccupied neglect that an artistic child lived with more acutely than his spontaneous drawing of his "family's mind-set" (see Drawing 8-11)? Equally adept, another youngster, wanting to show me more of his hidden thoughts, drew a boy and an X-ray closeup of what he carried around in his pocket (a prelude to his own opening up in treatment; see Drawing 8-12).

That how we treat and react to children's drawings makes a difference will take no clinician unawares. Open to reading everything and anything into what children draw, we are careful with what we do with this thinking. We do not report sexual abuse over one drawing of an evil-looking man (for, incidentally, we may learn in more cases than not that the child is portraying us). Nor do we jump in with twenty questions about the most provocative aspects of a drawing. We keep hunches to ourselves, probing or interpreting our suspicions only with caution and when an abundance of clues start to accumulate. Our overzealous trampling over children's drawings—as over their talking and playing—is the surest way to kill its displacing function, making drawing just one more place where the child feels unsafe.

> Seven-year-old Terrence showed me a picture of a child trying to win a ski race (see Drawing 8-13). "The winner gets his mother to give him a special snack," he explained. Although the mountain did appear to be somewhat of a breast, I refrained from saying so. When he asked me if I'd like to see a closeup of the "most wonderful mountain in the world," however, I said that I would, only to find clear confirmation of my speculation (see Drawing 8-14). These telling drawings catalyzed Terrence's more direct discussion of the longing for nurturance from a mother who was quite narcissistically unavailable.

Drawing, however much fun and appealing an activity, is no more or less than another realm in which the child can express herself within the therapy. As with any other precious thing the

Drawing 8-11

Looking in

7
magnified
+ x-ray
view of
pocket

Drawing 8–12

Drawing 8–13

Drawing 8–14

child says or plays out, what the child draws is subject to our careful observation and pursuit. Whatever the subject or manner of the drawing, we treat it as a communiqué, one whose meaning we will work to understand. As part and parcel of our relationship and the therapy, children's artwork is fair game for all of the vigilant watching, thinking about, and intervening that we as child therapists employ in our endeavor to help children know themselves better and more comfortably.

9

ALL TOGETHER NOW: BALANCING PLAY AND TALK

Children in therapy play. They also talk. While each in itself communicates and does the work of therapy, it is the interplay between them that endows play therapy with its richness and power. As therapists, how we deal with this sometimes vigorous, sometimes delicate balance is essential. How do children and therapists use the world of play and talk in therapy to their fullest?

Children vary in their capacities to talk and play. Some can play the dickens out of life and therapy. But they will avoid more direct discussion of themselves as if it were the plague that once decimated London. Other children talk easily but can't play. Some do both with ease and pleasure; some can do neither. What do these tendencies tell us and what should we do about them, if anything?

Seldom is a child's wish and ability to play a bad thing. Being a second and effective avenue for self-expression and communication, the gift of play generally makes play therapy easier and more appealing. Our play materials tell the playful girl immediately that this is her kind of place, and makes for a good beginning toward her ultimately taking ownership of the office and her therapy. We all know such children, and most of us feel encouraged when we meet them. These are the children who run to our toy boxes or spontaneously grab a dog puppet to bark at us when we've asked the first question they prefer not answering. Whatever the substance of therapy and its parallel relation to the matter of life, these children seem to get it even before we demonstrate it. "We're here to be with you," they appear to know, "and we can use whatever we want, however we want, to aid us in that endeavor."

Not every child sees toys as delicious invitations. Some perceive our playthings to be discomforting demands. The very playthings we hope will engage our patients can make some children feel they are in just one more place that will make them feel inadequate for not playing as a child should. That children who can't play are often uncomfortable interacting with people only accentuates their feeling out of place. And while making clear that children who don't want to or can't play are equally welcome here—staying put in our chairs, not trying to sell our toys too enthusiastically can provide some needed and early relief—it begs the question as to the larger picture of a whole therapy.

First-grader Jeff showed no interest in my toys. In his second hour he'd carefully surveyed them, but over the next several months didn't look at them again. There he sat for weeks of sessions, in the overstuffed chair across from my own, looking like a miniature adult—upright, rather still, and willing to discuss the reasons his mother had brought him to me.

A most serious and articulate only child, it was easy to see that Jeff carried the weight of the world on his smaller-than-average shoulders. His intellectual precocity and watchful nature, and his being parentified by an overwhelmed single mother, made for a child who knew too much, who was prematurely disillusioned, and who'd, to some degree, been losing out on the more innocent and free-living parts of childhood. Initially, when listening to Jeff talk about his difficulties, I wanted to throw him gleefully into the toy box. "Play! Play, little boy." But I knew that would have traumatized him; at least for the time being, he could not play.

Like two adults, we sat and talked of his worries about himself as well as his greater and justified worries concerning his mother. We talked about his contempt for children who do nothing but watch television, play videogames, and draw "stupid" pictures. He "had more important things to do," though he could never say what they were. Worrying, I suspect, was one of them. Our talking did help Jeff grow less worried, less tense, and considerably happier as well as more interested in playing on his own and with other children outside of therapy.

But Jeff didn't lay a hand on my toys until the last session of a planned termination. "You've got some pretty cool stuff," he noted as he rummaged through my toys. "It's too bad I never played with them." "And with me?" I asked, my remark causing Jeff to cry and nod his head.

"I wish my mom would have liked playing with me."

Jeff used his therapy essentially to talk through his not being able to play and his being raised by a mother whose own stresses and depression deprived him of the natural joy and responsiveness that makes for a good childhood. Each week's insights enabled him to play more freely outside the office and allowed him to take and enjoy the attentiveness that people other than his mother might offer. By not playing with me, by not indulging that longing, he constructively and unusually kept his therapeutic nose to the grindstone, analyzing, if you will, his frustrating plight right up to the final moment.

Conversely, there are children whose talent for fantasy and play, charming and intriguing as it is, proves somehow to bring less insight and progress than the wonder and passion of their hours would suggest.

"Satan boy" was a dramatic story that 10-year-old Gregory played for months. Each week the plot thickened, seeming to grow tighter and more to the emotional points that fueled it. Yet as far as we could see, there were no therapeutic benefits accompanying this play. Gregory left sessions appearing neither lighter nor heavier than when he came. School and the home front were status quo with bad news.

My attempts to move the play, enter it, or look at it were rebuffed reflexively. Like an eccentric cousin who won't let anyone get a word in edgewise, Gregory played at full speed, going around and under me as he needed, my presence more like an obstacle to the personal theater he staged. It was paradoxically only when, as a last ditch effort, I halted his play—before his parents halted the treatment—that his therapy took off.

"You can't do this," the formerly pleasant Gregory yelled. "I can do whatever I want in here. It's my hour."

I quietly stood my ground.

"It's my time. I don't care what you say. I'm playing anyway." Although Gregory protested loudly, he made no move toward the toys or "Satan boy." By the hour's end Gregory, having for most of it lambasted me with a sharp tongue worthy of "Satan boy" himself, was in tears. "You're no better than my parents. You don't care what I want. You only care about yourself."

When Gregory returned the following week he went right to work on "Satan boy" and I did nothing to stop him. We'd made an important transition together and he, though playing out the same fantasy, no longer had to lock me out. Having stated directly his smoldering sentiment, he no longer had to dedicate his play to passively denying me my watch and query, and denying himself the comfort and help of therapy.

The example of Gregory is one reason why I feel the humanistic child-centered view, though dear to the evolution and practice of child therapy, is in itself not quite enough. Establishing a safe atmosphere in which Gregory could be himself allowed him to play in his self-absorbed and controlling way, a way he would have continued forever, or at least for many more months, by which time his parents would have stopped bringing him. Providing an accepting environment in which he could blossom hadn't sufficed; exposing himself and his hurts was just too much. My standing in the way of his playing and interrupting his natural pace, steps that run contrary to the tenets of humanistic child therapy, were what pushed Gregory and his therapy onward.

Comparably we often meet children whose play moves so fast and wildly that we are at some loss concerning what it means and what we should do. These children, who often can fantasize with the prolificacy and terror of Stephen King's fiction, play, play, and play!

The play of Peter, an impulse ridden and occasionally psychotic third-grade boy, regularly resembled an epic nightmare staged by Hollywood of the '30s. For instance, in one hour "Cookie Man" stole all the cookies of the world (Peter was neglected and needy) mostly to deprive one little girl (he was also very jealous of his newborn sister) who was kidnapped by cannibals (oral aggression—biting, spitting, and cursing were problem behaviors) but didn't die because in the meanwhile Peter's attention turned to a village of stupid, happy people (Peter disdained peers he saw to be happy or earnest) that was being studied secretly by a mad scientist who appeared to be a caring man but really had evil intentions (me, his object of fear in addition to himself) and who was making a super nuclear bomb (Peter was acutely aware and frightened about America's situation with Iraq as well as his own colossal hostility) which went up into space until . . . .

This play occurred in a ten-minute span, if that. By the time Peter's right hand had set up some scene, his left was replacing it with another, this pace continuing, even accelerating, as the press of the hour's end came closer. Each conflict he played out engendered others, all of which, like hungry chicks, screeched for expression. So intense was the push of his internal world that the limitations of the external one mattered little. If Peter suddenly thought of death and needed a coffin, he'd grab the nearest object he could find. Unlike the child who wants every plaything to be in realistic proportion, Peter preferred to use a pencil as a coffin (to awkwardly lay a dead figure on) than to spend a moment searching for a box or making one. More acutely, it was less a matter of preference and more one of irrepressible need.

At first I tried entering his play world, but that soon failed miserably. By the time I got there, which was fairly quickly, his

play was somewhere else, causing me to literally and psychically miss
the boat. Remarking on the specifics of his play—"Cookie Man
sure is hungry"; "Cookie Man wants all the cookies for himself"—
went nowhere, for in the moments it took me to conceive and speak
my thoughts, his mind and issues had moved on. In a psychic form
of Heisenberg's Principle, Peter's play, his electron of fantasy, could
not be fixed in time and space. And if missing the mark weren't
bad enough, my fumbling intrusions only stressed him, giving him
even more feelings to have to bear and play out.

Much of what he did was incoherent and baffled me. There
were far too many characters too analyze, and each one, I knew,
was a most complicated mixture of people and projections. But it
would have been largely speculation and would have done nothing
to benefit Peter. Instead, I used talk, remarking on the process of
the play.

"Wow! So much happened and so quickly," I opted to say.

Peter sighed, seeming relieved by my simple comment. "It's
not easy playing like this," he added.

For months I sat back, saying but a few words each hour,
mostly at the end, words meant to capture the spirit of the whole
hour. "My gosh. Murder, cancer, kidnapping, babies born, babies
dying, schools exploding"; "Peter, it's astonishing. At 4:00 we started
in Boston and by 4:50 we'd traveled to every continent, outer space,
and inside a volcano." Peter listened intently to what I said. Gradually his play slowed, grew more cohesive, and employed fewer and
fewer figures, allowing me to play with him. After the first session
in which he invited me to play, Peter acknowledged that however
not-easy playing like this was, living like this was even harder.

The zest and whimsy of children's play, and our adult-centric
overvaluing of talk, can sometimes lead us to forget that what they
play can be as serious as what they speak, if not more so.

Barry was an exceedingly bright 11-year-old who suffered pervasive
anxiety and incapacitating phobias involving germs and illness. For
weeks he talked in a most pseudomature and emotionless way about

his fears. That discussion brought him no apparent relief. In the final minutes of his fifteenth hour, however, he nonchalantly made a toy woman drink from a tiny teacup, soon after which the woman died. "Your cup was probably poisoned," he explained. From here his therapy progressed steadily.

Barry seemed to speak about everything, everything except his greatest immediate fear, his fear that my toys were germ-ridden and that playing with them would make him sick and possibly kill him. But only through his small play gesture could he express that morbid worry and open the door to a resolution of his even bigger troubling thoughts and anxieties. For Barry, talk usually equaled an intellectual activity devoid of feeling. It was his play that ultimately allowed his worried fantasies to surface and be mastered.

Whereas the allure of rich fantasy play can make us forget the therapeutic need for discussion, play that is tedious and repetitive can lead us to push the child to talk more than is helpful or warranted.

"You be the truck and I'll be the car." Trevor had played this game for seven straight hours, each hour seeming to be a carbon copy of the last. "I'll crash into you and you crash into me." And so, for yet another hour, we did the same.

We might as well have been clicking ballpoint pens for fifty minutes once weekly, it seemed to me. I found myself dreading Trevor's hour. Clinically speaking, I couldn't see what I was doing to help him behaviorally or to advance his self-exploration.

In his eighth hour, after just a minute or two of his same old my-car-crash-your-car play, I pushed the cars aside. "What's bugging you?" I asked, thinking that my straight talk would glide through his guard, bringing his conflict to the forefront for our dismantling. But it didn't. Trevor began to cry, but not the kind of cry that is relieving or connecting. My assault on him had frightened him. Being with me in therapy was stressful enough. I'd pushed him over the edge. He spent the remainder of the hour withdrawn in a far corner of the office, unwilling to talk or to play.

"What had happened?" I found myself wondering as his next hour approached. I realized that my too-to-the-point query and decision that he and I must talk was not as much clinically guided as it reflected my hostility. "What's bugging *me*?" was the question that needed asking. I began to acknowledge how enormously irritated I felt when with him, particularly when he crashed his car into mine, feeling like someone who'd been getting head-slapped over and over again. Much more than boring me, he'd been passively shutting me out of his life and it bothered me.

> In his ninth hour I had the cars laid invitingly on the desk before his return. Armed with my self-understanding, Trevor's crash play no longer seemed to annoy me. It was no longer a personal thing. I recognized that he had to fend me off: closeness was the feared enemy. Reading accurately that he could play crashing as long as he wished and that it no longer bugged me, Trevor soon went onto more freed up play and talk.

The meaning of a child's playing or not playing, talking or not talking, is steeped in the finite context of the moment as well as in the child's bigger situation, in who the child is psychologically and the relativity of what the child is doing or not doing now compared with what she usually does and what she did last. Two spoken lines may be nothing more than a couple of grace notes for the child who talks nonstop through the therapy hours. For a second child, who tends only to play, those few words can speak a whole symphony.

A child's playing or talking can take on special meaning when its characteristic pattern changes. While playing board games can be a disheartening sign that one child continues to stall self-analysis, it can herald the good news that a second borderline and fantasy-fraught child's ego has grown sufficiently to allow him to sit peacefully and play a game. Similarly, while a tumultuous earthquake striking the dollhouse may just be one more instance of a violent child's play, it can be an indication that a neurotically inhibited child is getting better.

Short time-frame transitions between talk and play can carry meaning relative to the child.

> Stuart had worked hard for more than half an hour setting up a massive army of soldiers, townspeople, and policemen to battle my three large dinosaurs. Satisfied with the cast, he proceeded to play out a vicious battle that seesawed between the two forces. In less than five minutes only the T-Rex and the head general remained. Stuart raised the little soldier's right arm and sword and charged. But just before he could pierce the T-Rex, he abruptly put the toys down. "I'd better clean up," he said.
>
> "You've got almost fifteen minutes left," I said.
>
> "That's okay," he replied, his quick cleaning up telling me that he had some good reason for stopping.

Much in the way that conflicts disrupt analytic patients' free associations and motivation to do analysis, conflicts can disrupt a child's play and his motivation to do therapy. Only in the next hour did I learn what had halted Stuart. Reenacting the previous week's play, this time he focused on the duel between T-Rex and the general.

> "I didn't mean to kill you," the general cried, standing above the huge dinosaur that now lay on its side, dying with a sword through its head. "If you hadn't stolen my queen, none of this would have happened," the heartbroken general explained. "We could have been friends."

Though he liked his stepfather, Stuart didn't like the man's marrying his mother. Stuart's liking for him made him feel like a traitor to his birth father, a man who was far less adept at and invested in being a dad. Stuart couldn't play out such complex and heavy conflict easily and at once any more than an adult could tell it all during one therapy hour.

The reverse, of course, is something that happens all the time in child therapy. Ask a boy whether he is still getting many detentions and he suddenly has a burning desire to play dominoes. Sometimes the child is subtle, sometimes not. "Can't we just play?" "Do we have to talk?" Those less bound to civilities and decorum just walk away from us and our questions, playing as if we are nothing more than flies buzzing about to annoy them. Some children—those who not so incidentally are often less amenable to treatment—cut us off cleanly, closing themselves down to play apart from us and whatever we are evoking. Others, however much they try, can't do so and their play continues to deal with what it defends against, with what they are trying to run away from.

> Clark was in trouble. His private school was close to expelling him. His after school program had already done so. His defiance had alienated almost everyone in his life. Yet he refused to discuss any aspect of his situation, particularly his recent tendency to destroy whatever environment he was in. "I don't care," he muttered as he walked over to the toy box.
>
> But every dimension of Clark's play seemed to state that he cared very much. First, he made a big mess of the toys, dumping things everywhere in his attempt to find what he was looking for. Second, using play figures he staged a scene of a child who refused to use the toilet, pooping and peeing in the sink, in his parents' bed, and even on the Thanksgiving dinner. Third, at the hour's end the action figures voted not to clean up after themselves. Fourth, though I did not require it, he did clean up.

Clark's play essentially expressed with considerable complexity what he felt unable to put into words. Feeling empowered by my allowing him to defy my demand to talk, he began to show in his play the oppositional motive underlying his behavior. My allowing him to safely defile my office on many levels, to symbolically poop and pee on my office and myself, he was able to look at what he'd done and to decide spontaneously to clean up after himself. Through play like this he eventually grew to understand and master the fears evoked by his wish to be a good boy.

For many children, the displacing function of therapy—its allowing for more psychologically distanced expression of thoughts, feelings, and experiences—is well appreciated, if unconsciously, and naturally taken advantage of. But is displacement enough?

For some, like Austin, it is. Austin was referred to me after he'd been knocked off his bicycle by a neighborhood dog. The resulting phobia had increasingly closed his life in. He was afraid to leave his house, and that fear in turn induced a school phobia and also a reluctance to play with friends unless in his own home.

> With the exception of my initial evaluation, and only when I asked, Austin played and talked for four months without once bringing up dogs, dog bites, or his phobia. His play, however, overflowed with rage against his extremely controlling and angry mother. Relieving and coming to understand his own rage, the projection of which had made dogs look ominous indeed, quickly and surely undid his phobias. He left his therapy confident, his previous love of dogs wholly renewed.

Other children can play seemingly till the end of time without gaining insight, without making change, and without getting better.

> Although only 11, Jared already was rather abusive to his passive and depressed mother. Previous therapies, including family systems work and medication for his own depression, didn't help appreciably. Encouraged by his rich play and openness to fantasy, I eagerly worked with him for several months. Soon enough, I had to see that his playing out of abuse and strife was not helping. In fact, even after sessions in which he'd played out his mean-spirited behavior along with seemingly genuine remorse, he'd abuse his mother as they left my office.

Jared taught me that play alone, while important, is no cure-all. My work was no more helpful than the failed family work, for the same reason. Jared's parents were unable to stop their passive but sadistic treatment of each other and their torturous use of Jared as an object over which to wage their destructive and hateful war. Playing with me was merely sticking a pinky finger in a dam that was bursting with holes the size of basketballs. Sometimes a child's outer reality is so toxic that the child's playing it out can distract us from the harsher and bigger steps that must be taken or reckoned with.

Implicit in these discussions of talk and play is the question of whether to directly enter the child's fantasy world or to keep back and observe it. Although no guarantee of the right choice, children often tell us what they want.

> "Just watch. I'll let you know when I need you." Sitting on the floor, Erica kept her barnyard scene sheltered within her spread legs, her body shielding what she did. My slightest movement caused her to stop playing and to protectively circle her arms around her things.

Erica's behavior was not difficult to understand. Her mother was a destructively intrusive woman who, though quite sexually provocative, had never abused her. This mother routinely went through Erica's room and backpack in search of clues of drugs or sexual activity, believing she did it for her daughter's well-being. Erica welcomed the attention and help of therapy, but she feared that I would be as self-centered and manipulative as her mother. My allowing her to play safely and privately in my presence showed her firsthand that her complicated needs would be respected and met.

As much as Erica didn't want me intruding, Abby did.

> "Why aren't you playing?" Abby asked me with annoyance for the fifth time in this hour.

"I'm really frustrating you."

"Yes, you are. And I'm getting tired of it."

I chose to stop trying to explain to Abby the many reasons why I hadn't been playing. Because: she'd crawled under the chair, taking all of her toys with her; grabbed an action figure from me and told me to just shut up; switched the play so abruptly that I hadn't figured out what was happening in the split second it took her to complain that I wasn't there; she'd taken her play out to the waiting room, instructing me to wait in the office. Early in our meetings I learned that telling her why I wasn't playing only made her feel blamed, frustrating her even more. She wasn't interested in what she'd contributed to my not playing; she knew only that she didn't like it.

She had good reason not to like it. Her big-time banker father seldom spent time with Abby, nor did her equally big-time executive mother. Early on both confessed to me their "never being the kind of parents who play with their children." "Sometimes I'll read company reports while she plays next me," was how her father described their closer moments. "Children bore me," Abby's mother admitted. "It sounds awful, but that's just how I am." Was Abby responsible for her parents not playing with her, as she was with me? Not at all. What she constructively re-created with me were situations in which I was unavailable to her, and that abandonment was what she needed confirmed, understood, and help to cope with.

As therapists, especially with borderline and psychotic children—those for whom the boundaries between inner and outer reality are ill-defined—we often strive to put one foot in the reality of play while keeping the second firmly on the floor of external reality.

Nick was a severely troubled 8-year-old. Under the slightest stress he was prone to lose control of himself: throwing tantrums, destroying property, aggressing against others and himself, and urinating and defecating in his pants. Of even more concern was the degree to which he suffered from poor judgment, night terrors, and unremitting self-hatred that constantly put him in peril or invited mistreatment.

The cannibals—people action figures—surrounded the little boy who was being turned on a spit above the fire. "Help me! Don't let them eat me!" Nick screamed, sounding almost as frightened as any roasting child might feel. But things on this island were not as simple as we might have wished. "He deserves to be eaten. He deserves to be sliced like bacon and fed to the meanest pigs. But," he added, "even they will probably throw him up. That's how disgusting he is."

"But I don't deserve to die," I protested for the boy figure.

"You deserve worse," Nick replied firmly.

"But no child deserves to die," I said, hoping to side with whatever tidbit of self-loving protectiveness there was in Nick.

"No child but this one." Nick would have none of my sympathy for that child.

Nick made clear that I was not to save the boy or intervene in any other way. "What do I do?" I asked, meaning it.

"You watch and suffer like everyone else." And that's just what I did. Nick reportedly had a better week after this session.

Had I suggested directly that Nick was that child being cooked, he would have disagreed vehemently and felt stripped naked by my flippant exposé. A more tactful and psychologically cautious statement—"I wonder if you sometimes feel bad enough to be cooked and eaten"—would have injured him less but felt nearly as threatening. And beside, even if my remarks could be heard, weren't they awfully narrow?

After all, was Nick merely that boy? No. He was also partly the cannibals being punished for a voracious hunger for attention, admiration, love, and all of the other human food he had long been deprived of. He was also the chief cannibal who initially judged this boy as warranting that harsh consequence. This complicated mess was yet more complicated, for Nick's wish to wholly devour (and thus possess) those he loved and depended upon—while being punished—was also being gratified, for he, as the cannibals, got to enjoy the meal.

The overarching context between the two of us carried even more meanings. I was forced to helplessly watch the scene, confused and pained. Nick particularly appreciated my being witness to this multiply leveled, polyrepresentational drama, a concrete production of the psychic horror he bore by himself almost every moment of his life. Instead of making numerous pointed comments that connected bits and pieces of his play to himself, I interpreted in a larger way what I'd seen within the play itself.

"The poor boy. The poor cannibals. The poor pigs. Everyone is miserable and no one knows why any of this misery has to happen."

Nick understood what I said instantly and with satisfaction. Without stealing the cover of play from him, without prematurely confronting him, and without neglecting the most basic truth that the story was all about him, its sole writer, actor, and director, I conveyed that I grasped what he wanted most of all: my knowing just how bloody tortured it was to be Nick.

Using what I consciously knew about Nick, I made a superficially modest statement whose underbelly spoke to all of his various levels of conflict and hurt. By talking about the play creatures as I did, taking their plight and pain as seriously as I might that of human people, I helped anchor Nick in the outer world while helping to keep him safe and sound in his just-as-real inner world. It is playing in that transitional space, the realm of play and fantasy, that enables our child patients to learn to master and reconcile what they think, feel, and imagine on the inside with the stresses, truths, and limitations of the outer world they must live in and comply with.

The relationship between talk and play also can involve the relationship between affect and thinking. All cognition and logical

thinking won't do it, nor will waterfalling emotions that can neither be regulated nor processed. Children's play in treatment often,
though not always, involves more energy and spontaneity than their
talk does. How and why do we work to help the child connect the
two?

> Amy was a polite and cooperative child. She talked at length about
> her frustration at school and her wish not to go anymore. "I just
> don't feel right there," she explained calmly. "I don't know why."
> She spoke well only of the younger sister whom she regularly
> tormented. That tormenting plus the school phobia were the reasons
> her parents were seeking treatment for her. Any question I asked
> she answered, though her responses tended to be stilted and shallow.
>
> Amy's play was a wholly different species. Her murderous envy
> of her sister and the classmates with whom she had to share her
> teacher's attention came out loud, clear, and in brilliant technicolor.
> "I hate you. I hate you. I wish you were never born," she screamed
> at these competitors for the love she wanted to possess exclusively,
> her face beet red.
>
> "No wonder school is so terrible, "I said quietly.
>
> Amy nodded agreement, heartfelt tears cascading down her
> cheeks.

Many of the gains Amy made in treatment came from her
reuniting her emotional turmoil with her more rational thinking.
That allowed her to gain understanding that provided relief and
enabled her to make changes in her behavior, behavior that unbe-
knownst to her had been pushing away those she wanted close by.
Before treatment, her formidable brain power had enabled her to
adapt by relating intellectually to the world, her emotions coming
forward mostly when she was overwhelmed, when she could no
longer keep them to herself. As therapy proceeded, Amy's talk
became more expressive and revealing, as did her thinking; her play
grew less titanic. She came to live more comfortably between her

inner and outer worlds as a more integrated child who could flexibly both think and feel.

Arguably the most facilitating of all the intricacies between play and talk in therapy is the creation of a shared world that serves to hold, connect with, and invite children to face their lives and themselves.

> For months Maurice had built himself an entire world within the office. After experimenting with various arrangements, he'd settled on the desk as home base, the big chair becoming that of the enemy. The alcove was a magical escape hatch that offered unlimited supplies, all the information of the world, and perfect protection. When Maurice dared to leave our fort to see the world, he could enjoy all of those prizes by simply keeping even just a toe somewhere in the vicinity of that alcove. "Even atom bombs can't reach us here," he said. Within this general scene an abundance of complicated and evolving activity took place, which became increasingly organized and lasting. Each week took off where the previous one had ended.

Maurice used this ongoing play to cope with a life that was predictable only in its unpredictability. His parents were unreliable, however much they cared for him—indulgent this moment, neglectful the next dozen. Both parents had explosive tempers and waged horrific battles in front of Maurice. The elaborate universe he created with me allowed his therapy to move smoothly and efficiently, with no waste of time, enhancing its therapeutic coherence and efficiency.

Through such enduring play, or talk, children do their therapeutic work speedily and exuberantly. In fact, it can be a good sign when an obsessive boy decides that he neither wants nor needs to spend the first half of each hour recapping the one before or explaining to me every detail of what had gone before. "You remember," some children comment with surprise, happy that I care enough to listen and freed up to play more for themselves and less for me.

The pace and flow of a child's play and talk is as vital, varying, and interwoven as are the bubbling creek and the land through which it runs and percolates. It is our ongoing attention to talk and play, as well as the way they halt and ease one another, that allows us to most keenly help children to engage in their own therapy.

10

PUSHING THE ENVELOPE: ON GIVING, TELLING, AND OTHER EXCEPTIONS

If we've learned anything from our work as therapists, it's how critical are consistency and constancy. Our talents for playing, communicating, and understanding play second fiddle to our ability and willingness to establish and preserve the framework of the therapy. Still, whether or not in their own best interests, our patients yell for more, for things that run against or jump over those boundaries we've worked so hard to erect and maintain. We, being no less human than the children we see, know our own wishes to get around those walls—and not only in response to our patients' requests. What do these cries, theirs and ours, for exceptions to the rule mean, and what do we do with them?

The giving of things is probably the clearest place to begin our discussion. Early in my training I routinely gave my child patients gifts on their birthdays and during the holiday season. I did it mostly because my experienced patients would cannily tell me, the beginner, about the wonderful gifts their previous therapists had given them. "Give us something good and we'll like you as much," they seemed to say. "Or even more." My wish to make these unhappy children happy and the commonplace truth that grownups do buy children gifts helped to rationalize my relatively unexamined decision. Admittedly, the fact that I had only three child patients in that first practicum minimized the cost and inconvenience of buying presents. A caseload of twenty might have forced me to think through the clinical significance of my actions earlier.

My gift giving never seemed to accomplish what I'd intended. One child said a simple "Thanks" and then left the gift in my office. Another child spent his hour profusely thanking me for a gift that I could see disappointed him, and left more miserable than when he'd entered. My gift was a triple burden to him: not only had I given him something he didn't like, but because he liked me and appreciated my gesture, he had to keep his upset to himself; also, my beginning his birthday hour by giving him something took the wind out of his therapeutic sails. How could he dump his sadness and anger over his family's neglect of his birthday and him on someone nice enough to bring him a present?

What does it mean to a child to be given a gift by the therapist? It can mean the obvious, and generally what we wish to convey, that the therapist likes or even loves me enough to remember me in this way. This is perhaps something we want the child to feel as a so-called corrective experience. Clinically, this can most apply to the truly neglected child who also is unlikely to benefit from analyzing the lack of a therapist's gift.

Our presents can also send messages we don't intend. You've given me a gift, children can imagine, to make up for the fact that you don't know what you're doing with me; to bribe me or as a payoff for your failing me in other ways; 'cause you give gifts to everyone and so have to give me one, too; so you won't have to deal with my aggression; so you won't have to feel my sadness; because I nagged you for one; because you're too weak not to give me one; because you pity me . . .

As with everything else we do and say to them, children who misread why we've given them gifts can reveal more about themselves and their experiences than about ourselves. Those who feel the ways I've just described likely have good reasons to. Children who feel we give gifts to assuage their anger may have parents who do that, or perhaps that is their own modus operandi, the reason they give gifts. Projecting their own motives onto others, manipulative children can only assume we give presents, not out of pure generosity, but to get something (or not get something) for ourselves or to control someone. Children who have been reared to feel guilt for whatever they receive will be prone to feel in our giving the same underlying resentment they feel in their parents'.

Though they often misperceive our giving, children can sometimes detect the accurate, unconscious reasons for our giving. While we may think we're trying to brighten a poor child's Christmas, we may be trying more to alleviate our own guilt over the so-much-more that we have. Are clinicians who regularly give gifts to patients exceptionally caring, or are they unknowingly ensuring, by paying this tribute, that their patients like them or be happy? What does it mean when we find ourselves pulled to give gifts to certain children, not others? The more we can tease out the reasons for our gift giving, the less likely we will divert the therapy and the more likely we will allow for and recognize the impact of our giving on the child.

Whatever our underlying motivations, receiving gifts is apt to make children feel thought of, appreciated, appreciative, and to some extent indebted. "Are these feelings that will enhance the treatment?" we ask ourselves. A child who is respected, attended to, and cared for therapeutically might already feel all the feelings that our gift intends to bring. Will a gift add to them? Or will it detract? Being given a gift can discourage some children from sharing negative thoughts about us and the therapy, not just during the birthday session but for weeks to come. "If I can keep my bad feelings to myself," they may further decide, "my therapist will be more likely to buy me something else come the next occasion." And what does this gift mean for future months and years of treatment? Giving a

gift today can sometimes force a therapist into gift giving tomorrow; gift giving that feels right today may feel wholly out of clinical line in a therapeutic context that we and our patients have yet
to experience.

For all of our thoughtfulness, our gift giving or refraining can
lead to unexpected results.

"I don't want it." Six-year-old Colleen panted with upset, trying
to push the teddy bear back into its box as quickly as she could.
"Get it away from me. I hate it."

"You don't want the baby, either?" I asked, holding a smaller,
identical bear. Colleen's anguished screaming answered my question.
"Get them out of here!"

Adopted after a yearlong and traumatic orphaning in Asia,
Colleen experienced life as if skinless. To Colleen, daily living was
an endless ordeal of stress and injury. Whether coming from outside
or inside, almost every feeling threatened her self and typically led
to disorganizing pain and reflexive aggressing against others,
property, or herself. Having made considerable progress on her
capacity to attach with her most dependable mother, and very
connected with me and therapy, I'd hoped that the mother–baby
bear would be a perfect Christmas gift and a way to give her
something of me to keep when not with me.

Later that day, my wife saw me putting the bears into my car
trunk—I planned on donating them elsewhere—and wondered
whether I should keep them in case my patient should change her
mind. Although certain she never would, I put the boxes away.

Almost a year later, Colleen asked if I still had the bears. When
she heard that I did, she smiled but made it clear that she didn't
want them. Not until many months later did she ask to see them,
and only a year after that—following much therapy work around
the bears, centering on their being abused and abandoned themselves
—did she ask to take the mother bear home. As of this writing, the
baby bear still sits in its box, "orphaned for being a very naughty
bear," but safe with me under my desk.

Gift giving in reverse, though much less common, presents a variation on the theme. A patient's need to give to us is one that needs to be confronted, though gently.

"Open it," Elisa ordered. I opened the child-wrapped gift and found a fancy card covered with hearts and I-love-you's. "Do you like it?" Elisa asked anxiously.

"You've given me so much," I replied. And she had, ever since we'd first met five weeks before. "Let's see. There was the bookmark, and the mug. And then you gave me a lollipop and . . ." "Two other cards," Elisa interrupted. "And you made them all yourself. So much hard work," I said. "And for me!"

Elisa smiled with pleasure that I'd noticed all that she'd done.

Readers probably notice that I didn't reply with the expected and civil, "Yes, I like it very much." Why didn't I? Was I being cruel, I initially pondered, to deprive a sweet little girl of my approval, no less one trying to please me so hard? But feeling the compulsion of her giving counseled me otherwise. She was giving to me, it was clear, not because she loved me so much—how could she? She'd just met me—but because she had to. And that is why her gifts did not feel good in coming as much as they felt sad and frightened. But at that time Elisa herself didn't know for sure why she brought me presents. She learned why some weeks later when, having forgotten to pack her present from home, her mother reasonably refused to drive home to get it.

Absolutely panicked, and wanting desperately to make me a new gift right there on the spot, Elisa expressed her great fear that I'd be mad and not like her. Why wouldn't she, having a father—divorced and living states away—who could explode over almost anything, including a well-meaning and homemade present?

"You just want to make sure that I like you," I said. "Wouldn't you?" Elisa asked back. Yes, I nodded back. I would.

An overadoring tenor and frequency of gifts can also signal an idealized transference that needs some attention. While the patient's valuing of us and the treatment is generally favorable, it can lead to difficulties if unending in intensity and duration. This is especially likely when children can't acknowledge any imperfections on our part, yet find themselves extraordinarily critical of everyone else, even themselves, and whose life outside of therapy seems to be getting no better. A therapy full of nothing but love for the therapist is often rather empty and impotent.

I've seen other children whose regular gift giving was their way of asking me to give to them. In every instance my clarification of that wish has led to their no longer needing to give to me. And of course, in the majority of instances when, feeling good about therapy, they bring us a card or a Christmas gift they made, children expect and deserve a normal, human thank you.

The giving of food, or snacks, is an even more common aspect of child therapy. For some clinicians the giving of snacks is automatic either because of clinic policy—all child patients, for example, get to visit the snack closet—or personal belief that feeding children is part of the natural adult relationship with children. They may judge their child patients to actually need the nutrition of an after-school snack to maintain their attention in the hour. Or, understandably they may feel that this concrete feeding helps to relax the child or foster her good feelings toward the therapist and the work.

As one who occasionally but not routinely gives snacks, I find the giving of food to be one of those things we do at a particular time to give a particular child what she clinically needs, even if it's out of our usual therapeutic bounds.

Nine-year-old Heather, orphaned early in her infancy, was brought to treatment because of her explosive temper.

For months Heather showed me her finest moments, even stating, upon query, that she couldn't imagine anything I could do to get her angry the way so many other people seemed to do. Fortunately, this cheery prediction spoke more to the mounting resentment she feared would erupt even as she tried to suppress it. In plainer English, she soon blew, big-time.

After her rage passed, Heather began to experience a new feeling, an intense emptiness. She felt that she was a volcano that had spewed out everything inside, leaving a hollow cavity.

"I'm hungry," Heather said in a little voice. She rubbed her stomach as might a toddler.

"Would you like some cookies and milk?" I asked, deliberately using the words that so capture a parent's caring. Heather nodded that she would. She devoured the snack in seconds, looking like a child who hadn't eaten for days.

For months after that session Heather would ask for something to eat when she felt emotionally empty inside. She made it clear that physical hunger, not feeling the same, was an emptiness she could easily endure. It was the deeper sense of emptiness that was unbearable but that could be soothed somewhat by her requesting feeding and my obliging. I'd been tempted to unilaterally institute a weekly snack after the first one. But that would have diluted its specialness and dismissed her need. What would she do with a snack on days when she felt filled? What would she do on days she felt inordinately hungry? What might she ask for then, when the cookies and milk that were always there no longer eased the hurt deep within?

I readily offer snacks to children who complain of their stomach aching from more pedestrian forms of hunger just as I typically offer a glass of water to the child who's thirsty or a hard candy to another whose throat is dry from talking. I've brought out snacks to a child (and his parents) who had to leave home without breakfast because of a power outage. And I've provided a weekly snack for children who've come from homes that grossly lack any nurturing and who themselves lack the resources to do more insight-oriented therapy.

Much like the child who brings us gifts, we may encounter the child who brings two snacks—one for himself and one for us. Our response is best measured by what the child's gift intends as well as our own likes and needs.

> Maxwell slid a giant-sized soda and an even bigger bag of popcorn toward me while eating and drinking from his own. The third week in which he'd brought me food, I commented, "I wonder why you always bring me a snack," and readied myself for some guarded reply. Maxwell casually explained that he felt rude eating in front of me. "When I bring food to stuff your face, I don't have to feel bad about stuffing mine."

Although this dynamic did not turn out to be a central one in Maxwell's work, our bite-sized discussion enabled him to come to therapy with just one snack, saving him some effort and money. This also proved to him, he told me, that I, his therapist, could handle his being straight with me, a belief that promoted his being straight with himself when facing other topics.

The reasons children bring us snacks are as varied as the colors of their jelly beans. A second child who brought me weekly snacks, for example, had a much larger agenda than Maxwell. Raised by a single and alcoholic father whom he helped to care for, he felt obligated to parent me, too. In a majority of cases I've found that it was the parents, not the child, who felt the need to bring a snack for me along with one for their child.

When children offer us the occasional snack, do we eat it? One simple answer: it depends on whether we want to. Intuitively, doesn't it seem best to take the child's offering with thanks, eating it with gusto? Unfortunately, I find myself unable to do so. Sometimes I'm not hungry. Sometimes I don't like the snack. Sometimes I'm hungry and like the snack but am put off by the threads of Kleenex and pocket dust on the brownie, or I can't look past the just-up-the-nose or rear-end-scratching fingers that are delivering the cupcake. I've also learned the hard way never to eat foods that come from the hands of children with obvious colds and illness. It just isn't worth it.

When responding, we strive to see where the offer comes from. Responding either way to a no–big–deal kind of spur-of-the-moment offer is itself no big deal. The child hands us a stick of gum for no other reason than he's having one, has lots of them, and couldn't care less whether we take it. We are less nonchalant with children who appear or whom we know to care about the food they offer. Although I may not want to eat the opened string cheese that an isolated boy handed me—in his first positive overture to-ward me—I would not simply reject it, but make clear his gener-osity and my appreciation. I hesitate to take food gifts with the im-plication that I'll eat them later unless they are something I'll truly eat. Otherwise I set myself up for rejecting the child or having to lie—never therapeutically defensible—when next week he asks me how it tasted.

We frequently face our patients' requests for more involve-ment in their lives outside of treatment. They want us to buy Girl Scout cookies and raffle tickets and sponsor their walks for hunger. "Can you come to my baseball game?" they ask. "My school play is Friday night." Children naturally invite us to their homes to meet their pets, view their rooms, play their computer games, and eat dinner with their families. While these invites are usually qualified as needed opportunities to give me a chance to see their lives in the flesh—and in part they are—they more basically express the un-spoken longing that toddler patients express more openly. "Can you come live with me?"

What do we do with these requests? First, we must recognize that they are natural and to be expected. That they don't come more often is the bigger surprise and is probably evidence of children's somehow grasping that this relationship is different from the one they have with Aunt Betty or their lovely neighbors, the Dawsons. Why wouldn't children ask that we underwrite their efforts to sell more popcorn than every other Boy Scout? If we are so interested in their lives, their requests imply, why wouldn't we want to do our share, if not everything we can, to assist them in winning the award for being the troop's best salesman?

The nature of the request, that is, how it is delivered and in what context, often guides our response.

Bursting into my office, Carl slammed three candy bars onto my desk. "You owe me three dollars," he stated. "Well, pay up, you stingy bastard." He pushed the bars into my lap, frustrated by the few seconds of my not replying.

"I know you want me to buy some candy," I said. "But I don't know anything else about it."

"Forget it," Carl snapped. He then took the candy bars, smashed them against the desk, and threw them into the wastebasket.

From the couch on which he now lay and cried, he continued his hard if failing sell. "Now you owe me six dollars."

"Six?"

"Three for the candy bars you ruined and three for the candy bars you have to buy."

"For the bars I ruined?"

"You're a bitch," Carl screamed. "Why couldn't you just give me the three dollars so I wouldn't have to get so mad?"

My continued and steady posture of mostly just listening led to a torrent of revelations of the ways in which Carl felt unheard. By the hour's end he was able to laugh at the way he'd accosted me while describing his hatred of selling things.

"I wish someone would just buy me that knife [the reward for selling a certain number of bars]." He told of his nervousness ringing neighbors' doorbells and having to explain what he was selling and why. "I feel like a little beggar," he said, making his tough-guy salesmanship understandable.

At the hour's end Carl apologized for blaming me as he salvaged the candy bars out of the basket. Sensing the sincerity in his sorry, and having witnessed the hard work he'd done around the incident, I—above his insistence to the contrary—bought two of the candy bars. I held off from buying the third bar out of fear that my closing out the session too neatly would shut down the process that had just begun.

As we attend to the underlying motives in the child's asking for something, the right thing to do usually makes itself known and we can generally accomplish a good deal of therapeutic work. When a girl asks me to attend her championship soccer game, my patient and empathic confirming of her pride and her wish to share it with me will probably give her most of what she wants. When the child's want persists, we try to be frank but caring. "I know you want me to see your room, but I don't visit the homes of children I work with." Such a candid reply, especially when we understand just how rejecting our decline can feel, tends to lead to good outcomes; in that case, the child spent weeks drawing me blueprints of the rooms in her house, plans that she verbally annotated with important feeling and insight.

There are times, however, when we may decide to do what the child asks with a minimum of exploration. For example, I readily bought a church raffle ticket from a developmentally disabled child who, through this activity, was bravely going out into the world in a new and assertive way. I promptly backed an extremely self-centered child's participating in a run for a battered women's shelter, the first time I'd ever seen him seem to care about another person or cause. Likewise, when a most caring girl asked me to donate an old stuffed animal to her collection for a disadvantaged children's Christmas program, I saw no need to examine her motivations.

We try to beware of urgent requests that we don't understand. Hey-buddy-can-you-spare-a-dime, incidentally tossed out in the hour's final minute, can be deceiving, however noble or harmless it may sound. Why, I wonder, did the child wait until now? My generally unmoving position that I cannot respond to something that is unclear to me even if it means missing some deadline, though frustrating, tends to strengthen the child's growing sense of trust and reliance on the therapy.

Children, being children, are built to test the limits and framework of therapy and their therapists. "Do I have to leave now?" (Yes, unless there are very good reasons not to, such as a psychologically compelling line of thought or discussion that warrants extending the hour.) "Can I leave early?" (No, unless it appears that you are truly ill, or there is some very special event that you should be on time to, or you've already done some very difficult work today working on issues of closeness and staying will overwhelm you, spoiling the session's progress.) "Can we go outside?" (With me, generally no, unless there is something you wish to show me on the outside, such as your dog who waits in the car.) Every aspect of the therapy that is clearly firm and sacred the child will challenge to assess its integrity and ours.

"Have fun cleaning up," Lenice crowed at me as she headed for the door. A reckless 8-year-old who disrupted her home and classroom was now pushing my nose into her mess.

"You need to clean up," I calmly stated.

"What are you gonna do if I don't? Send me to bed without dinner? Tell my mother?"

Certain that I could not do the former, and knowing from earlier discussions that I would not do the latter, Lenice had drawn the line boldly between the two of us. This was our battle.

"If you don't pick up the blocks you won't get to use them next week," I replied.

"You wouldn't do that. Your job is to be nice to me."

"My job is to help you understand why you need to make a shambles everywhere you go."

Lenice smiled sheepishly, trying to look as if she could give a hoot, as she came back to clean up the room.

"Satisfied?" she asked provocatively as she kicked the last block across the floor.

"Lenice," I called to her in the waiting room. "You forgot one."

"You're a jerk," she muttered as she threw the one remaining block into the toy box before leaving with a slam of the door.

To have let Lenice off the hook would have played right into her delinquency-tempted hands. That she'd been coming to therapy for five weeks now suggested that she was ambivalent about her bad-girl lifestyle. Her testing me now underlined that suspicion. She was checking whether I could handle her. Could I, read the sequel, help her? My stubbornness concerning the last scrap of mess targeted her sociopathic streak. In the more wayward workings of her mind, were I to have overlooked that one measly block—what the heck, she cleaned up 99 percent of what she'd played with— she'd have beaten me, proving her badness and my unworthiness as the knight to tame her inner dragon.

If Lenice had been a well-meaning but disorganized child, I'd have helped her clean and said nothing about a block or two she'd missed. Were she a neurotic and overly self-critical child, I'd have said nothing, inside applauding her finally being able to make a mess without experiencing undue anxiety that I'd be mad or no longer like her.

The issue of to clean or not to clean can take an even more complicated form.

Tyler was an impulse-ridden, borderline 10-year-old who was still exquisitely vulnerable to stress from within and outside himself, though therapy had greatly decreased his susceptibility to psychotic regression. In recent months he'd come closer to acknowledging his frightful sense of himself as a worthless, perverted, and vile human being who deserved to die. This realization, while promising recovery, also threatened to do him in.

"Blah, blah, blah," Tyler repeated in a crazed monotone meant to annoy me. But seeing little disturbance in me, Tyler raised the ante and the volume. "I'm going to relieve my anus on you," he dared, describing in great deal how he'd defecate on me and my office.

Using the blocks, Tyler then built an elaborate outhouse in which he pretended to poop, this play contraption allowing him to exhibit his clothed rear end, relinquish (in fantasy) grownup control over his bowels, and poop all over me all the while in the containment and displacement of a play toilet. A very neat, creative, and important piece of therapeutic work, it appeared to me.

At the hour's end Tyler made one last noisy pretend bowel movement and walked to the door. "I'm not cleaning up," he said, teasing me but sounding ready to run back and clean up upon my expected demand that he do so.

"You made mess all over my office and you want me to clean it up?" I said with a smile.

Appreciating my good-natured acceptance—much in contrast with the harsher reactions he got from others in his life—he went to clean up on his own. But I gestured him away. "I'll be happy to clean your mess," I said. And I was.

Reading this account out of context could curl my own hair. How indulgent of me! Was I running the risk of inviting regression, leading a sick child to expect that he could find pleasure by relieving himself on me in his fantasy and play? Possibly, but Tyler's situation seemed to call for an exception in my usual framework.

Although coming in greater contact with his self-hatred—the basic precipitant of his self-destructive behavior and compulsion to repel those he seeks—he was not behaving worse. In his play he'd worked hard to create a wonderful play object, the toilet, in which to express his painful urges. My spontaneous willingness to clean up after him not only rewarded his good and higher-functioning play, it also symbolically held him like the mother who still loves her not-yet-toilet-trained and poop-covered baby, even after the Tyler-baby shows her the aggression and hatred that he habitually uses to assault himself.

Child patients not only want more things from us, they often want more information about us. Do we have children? Wives? Pets? Were we happy children? Were we naughty? Did our parents love us? Did they die? Where is our mommy right now? The questions can be abstract. "What are your views of the universe and its meaning?" Or practical: after I'd broken a pencil one toddler asked, "Will your daddy punish you after I leave?" Though infinitely varied in their content and construction, these questions all seek to better know and understand us as our child patients attempt to better know and understand their own families and themselves.

How much do we tell? Once more, it depends on the child, the circumstances, and our own need to reveal or be private. Occasionally we encounter conscienceless and violent children whom we tell little about our personal lives mostly because we don't feel that we can trust them. But in the more common circumstances in which we do not feel personally threatened by what children ask of us, we tend to examine their requests in terms of what makes clinical sense.

When our child patients ask if we have children, we look to know what they are asking. "Do you understand children?" "Do you know what it means to be a parent?" "Do you know what it means to love and care for a child?" "Do you let your children do things that my parents don't?" "Are you stricter with your children than my parents are with me?" And, of course, the most painful, relevant, and seldom articulated worry of them all: "Do you love *your* children more than you love me?"

We have no difficulty grasping a child's wish to know us better. After all, we are privy, or at least work to make ourselves privy, to the deepest and most inner parts of our child patients' thoughts, feelings, and experiences. "Tell us more," we sometimes must appear to be saying, while we sit like two-dimensional dummies behind soundproof and bulletproof Plexiglas. "What about you?" the children wish to yell. "Never mind, tell me more. Tell me anything about your humiliations, your failures, and your defects." This is one reason why children are so eager to sit in our seats, take our positions, and play the head honcho, the therapist who probes us, their patients.

Often our deciphering the hidden question in their questions does the trick, allowing us to provide the comfort or confirmation they need. "You wonder if I ever got into trouble, if I know what it's like to feel like a screwup?" "You wonder if I've known hard times or if it all came easy to me?" "You worry that I must love my children more than you."

Sometimes, what children most want us to see is that the one-wayness of therapy can feel unfair and frustrating. Children can ask personal questions that are motivated less by any specific interest than a more generic need to get us to say something, anything about who we are. And as we all know, children can ask questions about us as a counteroffensive ploy to steer the discomforting spotlight away from themselves.

> "Got any kids?" "How old?" "Boys?" "Girls?" "They like sports?" "They get into trouble?" "You ever hit them?"
>
> With the low key efficiency of "Dragnet," Gino asked me question after question. And I answered most of them.
>
> Knowing Gino and his family well from my work with a previous sibling, I didn't worry about sharing information with the 12-year-old. That he was interviewing me to ward off my doing the same to him was evident, but not problematic. In his scrutiny of me he more than revealed his own concerns as well as his prominent but long-denied wish to know his biological father, a man who had left the family when Gino was just a baby.

We all know moments when, in reply to a query or of our own accord, we deem it useful to disclose something personal that we hope will help a child patient.

> "What would you know about crazy thoughts?" the pretend-pooping Tyler declared.
>
> "We all have crazy thoughts."
>
> "You mean even you wanted to poop everywhere when you were a baby?"
>
> "Of course," I replied, assuming I must have.
>
> "No kidding," he said, satisfied.

I've shared with certain children my educational mishaps, moments of social embarrassment, moments of fear, and moments of great disappointment. Partly because of their rarity, our disclosures can carry special meaning for our children patients. While overuse of disclosure can wear out quickly (the child doesn't listen or it comes across as a competition of childhoods), used sparingly and wisely it can serve as a bridge to help children traverse especially hard experiences.

Although they may show interest in the facts themselves, any knowledge they glean about us tends to mean something. It is that meaning that we wish to see in order to help the therapy move as well as it can. When children learn that I have children, I want to know what that means to them and watch how they deal with it. "You're married," a young girl announces, just now seeming to notice my ring, though in her fourth month of treatment. "So what about it?" goes my gut reaction, a curiosity that, while not verbalized, leads to my observing and interacting around this issue for many hours to come.

Probably the most controversial and touchiest of framework strains is the child's (or therapist's) wish to give or take physical affection. Greater awareness by clinicians and consumers of sexual abuse, therapist misbehavior, and litigation has made the field sensitive, perhaps jumpy, around these most basic of matters.

To want to touch, pat, hold, hug, and kiss those we love goes without saying. That children want to do these things to us could not make more sense. If we show them all of the caring and respect to earn their most genuine trust and love, why would they not want to feel physically closer to us?

Leaving the obvious legal and ethical considerations to other books, let's focus on the clinical. To exaggerate the importance of the legal, subsumed by the clinician's self-interest, can cause us to misperceive clinical needs that run no risk of violating any child's trust or boundaries.

When a child suddenly and rarely shows us some affection—a quick and fleeting hug, leaning against us when showing us their wonderfully improved grades—it would be amiss, I think, to push the child away. As it would also be to pick the child up in our arms to prolong and deepen the embrace. We would calmly and comfortably, it is hoped, allow the child his expression, equally allowing him to retreat and go on with therapy, processing that physical contact only as he and the therapy judged to be necessary.

However, should a child want regular physical contact, we exercise a different kind of judgment, setting a limit with empathic caring for the child's likely feelings of rejection as well as inviting exploration of the longing that moved the child to ask for a physical show of love.

> "Do you care about me?" the bright 6-year-old Nellie asked, standing beside me.
>
> "Yes."
>
> "Do you *really* care about me?" she persisted.
>
> I nodded that I did.
>
> "Then how come you don't let me sit in your lap?" Nellie asked, her smiling face turning serious, her hand holding onto my knee.

That was a question I've faced with dozens of children. Sitting on the lap of the adults whom they love is part and parcel of their lives. It is the place they go for help, to be read to, to be told a story, and to be held.

> "You want to sit up here so badly. I know that."
>
> "Then why can't I?"

And why can't she? What's wrong with therapists showing their child patients that kind of caring? We often feel real love for our patients, so why not show it in real and concrete terms that a child can feel and understand?

"I don't allow the children I see to sit on my lap," I said softly but firmly.

"Oh," she said, still standing aside me, having pulled her hand off my leg to the chair's armrest.

I wanted my statement to make clear that it was my decision. "I can't allow children to sit on my lap" would be a bit of a lie, placing the blame on an outside authority, an agent Nellie would have been powerless to rile against. "Children don't sit on their therapists' lap" might be largely true, but it too would beg the question and push the responsibility away from me and the therapy. "It's not right for children to sit on their therapist's lap" would be worse, turning the child's reasonable and healthy request on its ears, suggesting now that she is somehow a bad girl for even desiring such contact.

"My grandfather let me," Nellie told me sadly.

"You miss him," I said, feeling no need to turn away the little hand that had come back to rest on my own.

Every child's wish to sit on our lap, or to be given affection in any other way, asks for love and security in its own unique fashion. Nellie's request revealed the longing for a beloved and recently deceased grandfather, one who, I'd been told, had loved her devotedly and well. Nellie didn't need my lap, a lap that would soon no longer be in her life. No, she needed my help in grieving a grandfather, doing so, moreover, with a mother who could not accept either her father's death or her own and her daughter's mourning.

In the once-in-a-while instances when a child, experiencing an epiphanal moment of pain or joy, clinically demands some affection, I would not push the child away; instead I'd permit the hug to come and go on its own. However, we are cautious about giving such affections on a more frequent basis, knowing that doing so may be confusing and may keep the child from doing the more important therapeutic work concerning the wish or need for hugs and kisses.

Some would argue that younger children need that kind of love. But it isn't true that such love is best coming from their therapists. And the argument that they are young is no argument at all. Younger children, particularly those who've been abused or come from seductive homes, can be just as confused by affection and physical attention. That argument also evokes a bigger question: At what age then would you pull back the hugs? Might a therapist hug a 6-year-old boy but push him away on his seventh birthday? If such dilemmas confuse us, imagine what they do to the child, especially to one whose experiences have made him even more vulnerable.

Even when we set the limit, however, we are careful to protect the longing and esteem of the child we've rejected. "I won't be hugging you," I've told more than one child with Down's syndrome—children whom the love of people has made extremely susceptible to exploitation—"but our hands can hug" (in a good handshake). While disliking my not giving them back a hug, and feeling much cooler about a handshake, these children have learned not only how to feel the love they want through my hand but how to deal more age-appropriately with others, to get more worthwhile attention, while minimizing the danger in their trusting social interactions.

And in times of physical pain I don't hesitate to do what I can. When Ethan's babysitter dropped him off at my office feeling sick and with his head cut, I did not need to question my prompt attention to providing first aid and comfort. I open windows and turn up the heat readily to keep my patients comfortable. For the children who, to my continued amazement, brave their way to therapy even when ill, I think nothing of tucking the office blanket over them or turning down the lights to soften their migraine. These children remind us palpably that there are many doable and safe ways to let our child patients know that we care.

The reasons we therapists break the rules are many. We may wish to please our patients so they will be happier, so they will like us, or so they will not be angry. Some clinicians might feel the press to please their patients so they will keep coming, keep being bill-paying customers. We also act out of unconscious pulls. Only by asking ourselves over and over, "Why am I being different with this child at this time?" can we ensure that we act out of clinical rightness and not to gratify or protect ourselves. Clinicians who truly intervene for their patient's best interests, not for self-serving ratio-nalizations, are in little danger of behaving illegally or unethically.

Like the wondrous jazz musician who must first master the basics in all their complexity, or the schoolteacher who must estab-lish her authority before she can ease the class into a happier and more self-controlled place, we must build our therapies on strong and dependable frameworks. Indeed, we can't afford to do other-wise. Ignoring the framework will nearly always lead to erratic, unreliable, and weak—if not abusive or dangerous—therapy expe-riences. Embracing it too rigidly, however, without room for nec-essary adaptions to the child's fluctuating needs, will forsake some of the most golden opportunities for therapeutic intervention and growth. We must remind ourselves that there are no absolute right or wrong answers. The right answers we seek are much more com-plex, variable, and changeable.

III

THE REST

11

HANDLE WITH CARE: WORKING WITH PARENTS

One of the most important truths of our work is also one of the most obvious: without a child there can be no child therapy. For the majority, it is parents or other caregivers who arrange for and bring children to our doorstep. Moreover, once a treatment is underway, its outcome hangs at least as much on what the parents do as it does on what transpires in the therapy office. Knowing so much is at stake, how can we best meet and enlist parents in our joint mission of helping them, as well as ourselves, to help their children?

Perhaps the first place to begin is to recognize that bringing one's child for therapy is generally a courageous and loving act. Entrusting our children to a kindergarten teacher, with all her familiarity, accountability, and public exposure, is hard enough. We can easily imagine how much more difficult and threatening it is to bring our children to someone who will meet with them in private to tamper with their minds and souls, while they along the way will likely reveal and confront our darkest and most regretted parenting moments. Yet this is sometimes forgotten when we find ourselves in conflict with parents or when we are feeling critical of ways they are treating our patients, their children.

We convey our understanding of this challenge by offering a compassionate and open ear to parents' stories and to what they have to say about their children, and by respecting their life choices. Although these choices may not be the same ones we would make, or even in their children's best interests, they are their own and for that reason alone need to be accepted and understood. Until parents feel that we care about the reasons they have gotten to where they are, or how they've lived, they won't often be open to changing their ways, particularly to ways that others, such as ourselves, have in mind.

We try to be honest. Honest about what we will be doing, honest about what we can and can't do. We present ourselves honestly, not just in terms of experience, training, and credentials, but with regard to our motives and perspective. If we are asked things we don't know, we say so. But when we do know things that need to be said, we say them, even when they're difficult. Despite their protests, I have met few parents or children who aren't willing to hear the truth if it is offered with respect, concern, and in the context of some hope—hope in the form of promising strategies or resources, however dismal the situation.

Through this combination of empathy, respect, and honesty we begin to build an alliance with the parents much like the one we build with our child patients. This growing relationship will serve many critical functions in the course of the child's treatment. Parents will feel good and trust us enough to enter their family to work with their child; they'll also feel sufficiently okay with spending their time, money, and hope on what we might do for them. As the relationship develops further, the growth of trust and mutual understanding will offset the inevitable misunderstandings or mistakes so that parents won't be as quick to pull the plug on the treatment or undermine it less indirectly.

That increasing well of positive feeling allows parents to reveal themselves with increasing candor. Their sensing that we don't see them as such awful parents ironically enables them to share and process the sometimes awful acts for which they feel ashamed or guilt-ridden. "That's nothing," many parents have indicated after mildly losing control with their children in my presence; "you should see me when I've really lost it." More times than not parents speak these words, not after I have put down what they did or insinuated that things must be worse at home, but after I've noted how much they dislike their own behavior or casually waited for their reactions. The liking and respect that parents feel for us, returning that which we give them, also becomes leverage that we will surely need to use at times in any therapy. In tougher therapeutic times, for example, when confronting even bigger, badder, or more painful circumstances and attitudes, we will need to draw on that accumulated positive relationship, like a rainy day account, to neutralize the hurt and rupturing influence of our interventions.

The dedication we share with parents to work on the child's behalf also provides a channel of communication for information. What is the problem? How precisely does it manifest itself at home, in school, and on the playground? When did it begin? What is the atmosphere at home like? Has there been abuse, neglect, or less startling trauma? How does bedtime go? Why did previous therapies work or fail? Parents can give us the data we need on current circumstances, family history, development, and every aspect of their child's life and background.

The importance of parents' filling us in applies not just to the evaluation phase but to the treatment in its entirety. There are unusual children who are able and willing to talk about matters that most trouble them and others; many more try to avoid such areas for as long as they can, or forever. The notion of children blossoming in the safe and nurturing arms of therapy is a lovely one, but most children, like most grown people, tend to turn away from painful and difficult parts of their lives unless somehow pushed or otherwise motivated. If it were not for the parents telling me, I might never know that a child has been failing three subjects, lighting fires, talking of suicide, or experiencing the countless other problems that require attention in therapy.

Parents often need our training, particularly early in a treatment, to keep us informed. Although the big blocks of material they
give us early on are important, it's apt to be the week-by-week
updates that alert us to the relevant events and reactions occurring
in the child's life.

"Anything I should know?" I often ask casually of the parent
who's taken a seat in the waiting room. Parents learn that by *anything* I mean whatever concerns them, needs to be known, or might
facilitate the day's therapy. It's here that parents tell me of upcoming doctor visits that their child is obsessing over, increased aggression or sibling rivalry at home, calls from school, or the child's
uncharacteristic attempt to avoid coming to the session that day.
This information can frankly give meaning to a stale hour, particularly as children are prone to avoid matters they're trying not to
feel or think about. Most parents quickly learn how to use this space
around a child's hour to efficiently communicate.

I similarly invite and usually urge parents to use my answering
machine to leave me bulletins reporting an upsetting moment, a
good example of a current problem, or a troubling passing comment (e.g., "I'm never going to amount to anything!"). Encouraged not to worry about leaving an extensive or elegant message—
"just blurt out what's happening"—parents become skilled at telling
us what we need to know. Knowing this route is open to them,
I've found, makes parents a bit more observant of their child and
their own parenting, resulting in better parenting behavior. This
arrangement may sound onerous to the clinician, but it actually eases
our work, allowing us to help children and their parents more
quickly and clearly.

But getting information on the sly from parents raises its own
issues. I try to make clear to child patients my request for parents to
keep me informed. Most children don't seem to mind. While parents often cringe initially at my suggestion to openly let their children know of our communications, they soon learn that it isn't so
traumatic. Having our contact out in the open allows us to bring

up the topics directly—"I heard about your dog [dying]" or "You know your mom told me about the suspension on Friday"—should they not do so themselves in a therapeutically timely enough fashion. More times than not, we don't need to make specific mention of what we learn. Our simply knowing gives us a context in which to decipher what we see and hear in the session.

Parents also gain finesse at bringing up matters in a way that moves a child's work along, especially around small but critical junctures. They learn to catch our eye or ask if we think it advisable that they tell us something. "Do you think it makes sense to just come in for a few moments?" I'll ask. When parents think it does, they usually have good reasons. These mini child–parent sessions, occasionally expanding to an hour but more routinely lasting minutes, can propel some of the deepest and most difficult work we do with the child.

Unsurprisingly, there are times and parents that require a variation on this theme of access. Some parents never call and share little information around their child's hour, letting us know at their meetings and only after too much time and to our enormous frustration that things are no better or worse than ever, moving us to invoke a communication initiative a bit more forcefully. Other parents need our influence in the other direction.

"He screamed at me all morning. He didn't clean up his room when I asked him to. And," she added, as her son, Carlos, sat across from me, quietly listening, "he's been walking around the house with a major attitude." When she left the office I looked at Carlos, my eyes asking him what he thought of all his mother had said. Just as he began to tell me, with an abrupt knock and sudden opening of the door, she stuck her head back through the door. "Oh, and I'm not sure we like some of the kids he's been hanging around with either."

After she left again, Carlos rolled his eyes. "She always does this," he said. "She talks about me to anyone who'll listen." Carlos described how his mother habitually gave detailed reports of his misbehaviors to his father, her friends, and his grandparents. "I understand why she gets upset sometimes," he explained, "but does she have to tell the whole world about it?"

Carlos's mother meant well, but she meant other things, too. When she wasn't filling me in on her son's failings, she was reporting on those of her husband and her aging parents.

It was clear that Carlos's mother felt let down by almost all of the important persons in her life. Once I made clear my understanding of this—which I did outside her son's presence, at an hour's end after he'd run to the car—I could ask her how it must feel for her son to hear her speak so harshly of him in front of me. She easily grasped my message. This question of family dynamics continued to be one that we worked on in parent meetings. Why did she need to put her son, and others, down so much? In the meantime she came up with more constructive means of sharing useful information with me.

Parents, particularly early in treatment, tend to see our communicating as intended to convey the dirt, the ways in which their child's or their own behavior has gone awry. Gradually, often with our help, they come to see the value of also sharing good news. These more upbeat updates may apply to big goodies, such as a markedly improved report card or complete disappearance of a nasty behavior. But it is more important that parents be led to report the teeny steps that over time amount to therapeutic progress.

"Things were okay," Mr. Toyo replied dismissively in response to my asking how their Sunday family day had been. "But when we returned the canoes," he continued, his voice growing louder, "Kyle just lost it. Sara was handing Kyle their paddles, and—"

"Kyle went canoeing?" I interrupted to ask, having heard so many times about his utter dread and rejection of the very water sports his father loved.

"Yeah," Mr. Toyo answered, seeming to be caught momentarily by what he'd failed to notice, "but it was just a shallow lake. It wasn't as if we sailed out in the ocean."

I was tempted to pounce on that, to point out Mr. Toyo's impossible demands of his son, but the slight hesitation caused me to wait. "Gee, that must have been a pretty big thing for Kyle, don't you think?" Mr. Toyo asked.

I nodded my agreement.

"But anyway, when Sara handed Kyle their paddles—"

"*Their* paddles?" I asked, again cutting him off.

"Yeah, they shared a canoe."

I looked Mr. Toyo in the eyes and he immediately caught my drift. "They don't usually do things together, do they?"

I smiled.

"Maybe the day was better than I recognized."

Getting it, Mr. Toyo was then able to describe what he'd origi- nally wished to, his continuing frustration with Kyle's behavior. My gently urging him to see the little giant steps that Kyle had taken buoyed Mr. Toyo, warned him of the ways in which he, always so aware of his son's shortcomings, failed to notice his achievements, and led to his giving Kyle more praise and credit for such shows of bravery and change. Not surprisingly, this modest discussion began Mr. Toyo's own exploration of the ways in which he acted as criti- cal and unimpressible as his own father had. Encouraging parents to share these miniature victories can foster their being more atten- tive and observant of their child's efforts and accomplishments, give them week-by-week encouragement as they wait for the larger therapeutic rewards, and make them more aware and proud of their every step forward at parenting.

The information turnpike that runs between us and parents does even more. Establishing this hot line helps to make parents feel held when they are not in our office or waiting room. It helps parents feel less alone with their troubles, reduces the likelihood that they will somehow sabotage or undo therapy due to frustra- tion and resistance, facilitates their positively attaching to us, and lends them ego support for withstanding the stresses of their home lives.

We establish this communication, this relationship, with parents in the service of achieving therapeutic goals with their children, our primary patients. For many, parenting well is not as natural a process as some would like us to think. One of our chief objectives is for the parents to come to appreciate where the child is and what she needs, from many different aspects.

Where is the child developmentally? For example, what is the developmental meaning of a child who often cries for her pacifier? If the child is one year old, it is as it should be. If the child is 3 years old and otherwise quite normal, we may together discover that her not wanting to give up her nucky has intensified since beginning preschool. Regressing at the age of 5 years old and crying for the pacifier she spontaneously gave up at age 2 could relate to the recent birth of a baby brother. An 8-year-old's buying herself a pacifier and using it secretly may be giving a message to parents who, fearful of overdependence, forcibly weaned her of all sucking early in the first year. And while interest in the pacifier can signal an untoward reaction to stress in a well-loved child, it can be a sign of growth, of openness to attachment and nurturance, in a neglected and hardened child.

Seeing the developmental context of the child, particularly that in which troubling symptoms or behaviors occur, is critical in determining what we should do. We reassure the young parents who worry, making clear that their instinct to allow their baby to suck all she wants is a good one. We help the 3-year-old and her parents cope with her separating to preschool, a decision about which the parents felt ambivalent, even guilty. We play with the 5-year-old who, having a good home and able parents, must grieve the changes that having a sibling brings, helping her parents to see her regression as something natural, not to be squelched, and that would pass. Deeply understanding the feeling that drove the 8-year-old to buy her own pacifier, we help her to better understand her dependency and oral needs as well as the hurt inflicted by her parents' well-intentioned deprivation, just as we work with her parents to see the reasons they have such reservations and discomfort about nurturing their child. With the loved child who is regressing, we take her stress seriously, working to resolve it externally as well as to enable her to withstand it better. But for the child who had nearly given up on humanity, we may do little more than celebrate and nurture his allowing himself the pleasure of a suck.

Helping parents to know where their child is intellectually, emotionally, socially, and the rest, and how the reasons for referral fit into that picture, implicitly helps them to understand what we do or don't do in treatment. That knowledge, like most, will take some of the mysterious fear out of their relationship with their child, giving them data from which they can now make informed and more effective choices. It may propel parents to become active in ways long overdue (e.g., raising expectations for the child) or to chill out (e.g., not assess every moment of the child's life), making more comfortable space for their child to be and grow. What parents come to learn can alleviate worry and remorse, as when they realize that their child's state is a transitional and natural developmental phase. It can also be quite painful, as when a father comes to see how his limitations and misparenting have caused his child unnecessary hurt and hardship.

Closely tied to development is the question of temperament. If developmental research has taught us anything it is that children are all born different. Some infants are bold, some timid, some curious, some active, some passive, some affable, some cranky, some stoic, some sensitive. Infants, temperamentally speaking, come in all shapes and sizes. Part of our role as child therapists is to help parents recognize and accept who their child is temperamentally. While it is debatable whether one can wholly reverse a child's development, and even more debatable whether one should, how parents' temperaments interact with their children's has a great effect.

If I learn that a boy is quite shy, for example, I can help parents recognize that they unduly push him into situations that overwhelm him or make him feel less loved and worthy than his older sister who so easily takes center stage. Conversely, I sometimes recommend strategies to help parents respond to their child's temperament, showing how that same child might benefit from gentle urging to pursue activities or not to be treated with such kid gloves.

Issues of the child's temperament often connect directly with issues of a parent's temperament.

"I don't know what to do with him anymore." Mrs. Ellsworth spoke confidently and with disgust. Her 9-year-old Sam stood at the window, looking outward. "It was his birthday and he barely had fun. All of the other children were screaming and running around the house, having a complete blast."

"Eric wasn't," Sam interjected. "He was—"

But his mother interrupted. "Eric was up and down the tree house at least a dozen times when he wasn't diving in the pool. Does he take diving lessons?" Mrs. Ellsworth asked, seeming to forget her irritation for the moment.

Sam said nothing.

"I sign you up for tennis, soccer, kayaking, but it never grabs you." Then she spoke to me, as if delivering her case to the judge and expecting me to affirm her disapproval. "All Sam wants to do is read and do whatever it is he does out in the yard."

"You sign me up for activities you want me to do, not things I like. You wanted a great athlete for a son, someone you can ski with on weekends and show off at the club. Well, I know you're disappointed, but I'm not that son. And what I do outside is not whatever. I study nature and wildlife."

"He's obsessed with drawing pictures of mushrooms and flowers."

"Is he good at it?" I asked her.

Seeing his mother lost for an answer, Sam chimed in. "She's never looked at them."

Sam was quite right. His mother, a fine athlete, had wanted a son to share her love of sports. She envied the mothers of the confident boys who played golf and tennis at their country club. Her son's preference for quiet and intellectual pursuit repelled her. While our work together didn't change the basic nature of either Sam or his mother, it helped her to see how his being so different from her frustrated and upset her, and led to her misparenting him.

Such mismatches in temperament are common. Bold parents who dislike their child's quietness. Inhibited parents who don't know where that exhibitionist of a son came from. Fearful parents whose brave children hold their hands at the doctor's or who provocatively drag them to the roller coaster. Discovering how their own temperaments affect their perception of their child's can make a difference. It reduces parents' bewilderment and dislike of who their child is and with that the risk that they will intervene in ways that either ignore the child's potential for growth or push him to climb cliffs beyond his capacities.

Although we tend to encounter the families only after the child is several years old, their asynchronies in temperament start impacting on them from birth. A mother able to wholly console and nurture her firstborn may find her extremely active and irritable second child much too much, his edgy personality so at odds with her own. Day by day, the frustration that results at either end of the relationship can lead to major misparenting and hurt for both parent and child. Coming to understand the tension of that mismatch at a later stage of childhood can prove helpful and reparative, even though the truth does hurt.

While some referring problems reflect innate aspects of the child's functioning (anxiety or learning problems based mostly, if not completely, on neurobiology), others originate out of psychodynamics. As the therapy unravels these dynamics and illustrates dysfunctional patterns, we enlighten parents about what their child's symptoms or misbehaviors mean, what psychological functions they serve, for the child as an individual or the family as a whole.

Scott was a sixth-grader with intelligence solidly above average. Yet he had been doing increasingly poorly over the academic year, receiving four D's on his last report card. His teacher observed that he "had to work hard" to do so poorly, knowing that even the most minimal effort and cooperation would have brought higher grades to a boy as bright as he. Scott's deteriorating grades greatly distressed his parents, both of whom had professional degrees.

Over months of therapy Scott came to understand that he had indeed unconsciously worked hard to not do well. His not handing in homework, not listening to assignments or instruction, and not paying attention to what he read were not motivated by an inherent neurological or learning disorder; Scott simply resented his parents' exaggerated and singular investment in academic achievement.

His parents, preoccupied with their work, had little time for him, and when they did they used it to scrutinize his school performance. There was little fun in the house—no television, no sports; reading was designated as the home's official outlet for relaxation. Learning left Scott feeling cold and empty, burdened with the need to achieve and lacking good feeling, particularly when he compared what went on at friends' livelier, less intellectual homes with what happened in his own.

Our deciphering the good reasons for Scott's hostility toward school and learning enabled him to make better and less self-spiting decisions on his own behalf. Of equal import, clarifying his behavior for his parents moved them to examine themselves, their parenting, and their relationship to their work. Their confirmation that his feelings were justified—that they ignored him and much of life in favor of their work, as he accused—freed Scott to express his intellectual potential as he saw fit.

Just as we strive to demystify our child patients' anxiety, pessimism, suspicion, mistrust, fear, and shame for both them and their parents' edification, we try to clarify the sources of their small behaviors. "Matt snapped at you [his father] because he felt belittled by your laughing [when he tried, with pride, to tell of the ways he helped you work in the yard over the weekend]." "Ivy isn't talking with me because she believes you [her mother] will be hurt if she complains about you [in therapy]." "Caitlin [a supreme worrier] hasn't been eating the past few days on account of hearing a news report about tainted food poisonings."

Our disclosing what's behind their child's behavior or symptoms holds much utilitarian value for parents. Discovering the psychological functions these behaviors serve can minimize parents' taking it all personally. Their child, they grasp, does this or that, not mostly to irritate or oppose them, but to protect his own psyche, to make life bearable and doable. Unchained from their retaliative imperatives, they may find themselves more able and willing to parent in ways that promote their child on his self-directed recovery.

A counterpoint to helping parents understand their children's motives is helping them uncover their own.

"I don't care what you do, just fix him," Dr. Jamison said to me, meaning it. He referred to his 9-year-old son, Zachary, a hellion on two legs. Zack was everything his 66-year-old father was not. Dr. Jamison, a professor of history, was highly cerebral, unathletic, and deliberate in his motion. Although bright, Zack had little interest in books, much preferring to be in action of almost any kind—as long as it was high speed and fun.

Our work soon came to focus on Dr. Jamison, a reluctant father who was more than satisfied with having raised three grown children from two previous marriages. He had brought Zack to me with a mandate to calm him down quickly, using drugs if necessary, but Dr. Jamison confessed, with not much coaxing, his worry of growing older, noting how Zack's boyish enthusiasm and energy only made him feel that much older and slower. It also brought to the forefront Dr. Jamison's regret that he'd not been there for any of his children and his awareness that he was much more at home with books and ideas than with real people, even people he loved. He acknowledged that he'd never been a robust person, even as a boy, and that his whole life he'd harbored envy for those pursuing a more vigorous existence.

These insights led to Dr. Jamison's growing less critical of Zack's healthy robustness, and to a rapidly growing mutual interest in each other's lives, Dr. Jamison cheering Zack on athletically and Zack hanging around his father's reading room.

There is much therapeutic reward in advancing parents' learning what they really think and feel about themselves, their child, and their parenting. But this work is fraught with pain and regret. We all want to believe that we hold nothing but good feeling and thoughts for our children, so confessing one's unconscious hatred for a child is one of the hardest things for a loving parent to do. Admitting fear of separating from one's children, jealousy or envy of them, and ambivalence toward them does not come easy.

Therapists aspire, moreover, to reveal how what parents do sometimes serves to protect their own esteem or tries to repair and compensate for hurts and neglects in their own childhoods or adult lives.

Our work with parents in this regard typically runs slowly and carefully. Rather than hammer parents on the head with instances of their misperceptions and misparenting, we—by listening, being safe, and intervening aptly—seek to create the atmosphere and right amount of tension that leads parents to confront themselves. Instead of blasting and shaming them, we attempt to hold them as they whip themselves, keeping them afloat and hopeful even as they feel themselves sinking under the weight of their anguished revelations. (This latter part shouldn't be unduly hard for us, for however gloomy and self-hating their words, it is almost always encouraging when parents own up to their misparenting.)

Associated with the goal of parents' knowing themselves better is that of fostering their interest in and capacity for taking their child's perspective. Sometimes we foster this by extrapolating to the parent's adult life. "Imagine what it would feel like," I said to one father, "if your wife came home one day and said, all excited, 'Honey, guess what? I so enjoy loving you that I've brought home a second husband so we can be an even happier family.'" This analogy, heavy-handed and probably overused as it was, moved this father beyond his intolerance for his daughter's regressed reaction to the birth of a new sister. To make the child's situation and feelings more vivid for a parent, drawing comparisons between school and the work place, adult ideals and childhood dreams, and the parent's and child's childhoods (i.e., intergenerational dynamics) can work wonders.

Unfortunately, some parents are just so far from their child's world, or so defended, that our work needs to be less ambitious. "I know it's hard to understand how Timmy can be so afraid of the school bus," I gently said to one father, conveying that I understood his frustration. "But he is afraid, very afraid, so what can we do to help him grow braver?" Timmy's father was not ready to examine his own counterphobic daredevilry and how it affected his son; he was prepared, though, to work constructively on helping his son overcome his fears.

Implicit in the goal of parents' taking their child's perspective is their taking seriously the impact their own behaviors, words, and demeanor have on their child. Most parents take for granted the ways they parent, even ways that may be harmful or waste energy and time. And so we carefully cite their behavior or demeanor. "Is Shawna the only one in the family who's quick to criticize?" I ask of parents I know to be critical. Similarly, we urge parents to consider the effect on their child of their passivity, their impulsivity, or their always needing to be right.

Some of this work occurs in the transferencelike relationship that evolves between parent and therapist. "What's it like for you to see my family?" I asked one mother who could not understand her daughter's envy of my children. My query evoked the mother's saddened fantasy that her family would never be as joyous and loving as she imagined mine to be. In another instance a father complained, "My son's so unable to take criticism," only minutes before he himself had felt insulted by a remark of mine. When we noted the connection, this father discovered lines between his own narcissistic vulnerability and his son's.

As therapists, we hope that seeing the influence of their misparenting will deter parents, yet many, even after realizing its effects, continue their marital battling, drinking, or other serious indulgences. In such cases we at least work toward preventing the risk of parents' punishing their children doubly by adding the burden of secondary blame to the original behavior. Growing up with alcoholic parents, for example, is beyond awful, but it is even more awful for those parents to blame their child for their drinking or to deny the reality the child sees accurately.

As child therapists, we of course do much parent guidance. We may educate parents about what children of that age, ilk, gender, circumstance, and so forth are like. We help them to see their child's need for love and discipline and we provide instruction on limits and consistency. We try to reduce stress and to introduce methods to cope with stress that can't be avoided. We offer reassurance when we can do so honestly, and we hold parents' hands when they are frightened and shaky.

We offer all the help we possibly can so that parents can create a home atmosphere most conducive to the child's progress in therapy. Parents who put out the money and effort to bring their child to us generally want to help catalyze therapeutic gains. And we don't mind giving bits of advice, together with our big explanations of what is going on, to move things along in the family or remove roadblocks to the child's healthful momentum. To that end we prepare parents for what might happen. Such predictions can take the edge off potentially noxious behavior.

"Lorrie may become a lot more outspoken and ornery as he grows less inhibited," I warn, using interesting adjectives that connote something more intriguing than might the words *rude* and *crude*. And Lorrie sure did. But anticipating this obnoxious change helped

Lorrie's parents to understand it as growth on the road toward greater confidence. Quietly encouraged by it, they felt no impetus to punish Lorrie or even make their own noise about his.

Putting a child's change into a therapeutic and developmental context, provided that it belongs there, can provide parents the support, inspiration, and principles they need to make room for their child's growth. Such explanations go miles toward preventing them from making well-intentioned attempts to stop tears, tantrums, outbursts, and withdrawal, any or all of which might be temporarily necessary to the child's ongoing development.

Throughout this work with parents we show them—by keeping our doors open, making their input and observations welcome, and respecting their undeniable sovereignty as the parents who love their child best of all—how we and therapy work. Rather than merely tell them what we do (though that has its place), we demonstrate it in the office, in the waiting room, on the phone, and in between. Ever remembering how bad bringing one's child to therapy can make parents feel, we try to bring insights or make recommendations as subtly and nonthreateningly as we can. We watch for signs of narcissistic injury and encourage parents to share with us frustrations and anger that we have caused them. Whatever we think of our helpfulness and skill, we make clear that it is the parents' privilege, if not obligation, to alert us to their disappointment or disapproval of what we and therapy are doing or not doing.

In short, moment by moment, incident by incident, misunderstanding by misunderstanding, and session by session, our connection with parents builds, slowly but steadily, growing ever stronger and more effective through to our final hour with them and their child.

12

HARD TIMES: UNWILLING PATIENTS AND THERAPEUTIC CRISES

Few worthwhile enterprises come easy, and child therapy isn't one of them. Pain, doubt, and royal messes tend to accompany almost every substantial course of therapy. That some of our patients find themselves less than enthusiastic about treatment should come as no shock, nor should the fact that many also experience crisis points along the way. This chapter explores both hazards as they apply to child psychotherapy.

UNWILLING PATIENTS

Many onlookers assume that play therapy offers children little more than unbounded play and self-expression under the celebrating eyes of a therapist. Although the kindness, understanding, and tolerance of therapy can be pleasurable—and can themselves be healing and growth advancing—much about child therapy is not at all pleasant for children. Contrary to more naive and devaluing beliefs about our work, child therapists do much more than just play with chil-

dren. We escort them on their journeys toward self-discovery and
self-revision, journeys that often take the child through anguished,
humiliating, frightening, uncertain territory. We essentially ask them,
no less than our adult patients, to examine themselves—their misbehaviors, their bad attitudes, their greatest anxieties, their deepest
and darkest thoughts, their most hidden and precious dreams.
Frankly, given the awesome nature of what therapy asks of the child,
I am struck that more children don't find themselves reluctant to
engage in therapy.

> "Nice day, isn't it?"
> An unusual comment for an 11-year-old boy, it would have
> been civil enough if it hadn't been the umpteenth time he'd said it
> this first hour. For that matter, "Nice day, isn't it?" had been the
> only thing Dana had said for the first forty-eight or so minutes.
> Although spoken in a friendly tone with no hint of sarcasm, its being
> repeated as the answer to questions about himself, his life, and his
> being here betrayed its resentful purpose: letting me know that Dana
> did not want to be in therapy.

Wouldn't it have been easier if Dana had just told me that he
didn't want to be there? At least we could have talked about that
directly. But Dana, understandably, did not feel safe enough with
me to share his feeling openly. As it was, and despite himself, he
showed some of himself—as we all can't help but do—by expressing his opposition in a passive and seemingly untouchable manner.
He had been suspended from school several times and frequently
had equivalent difficulties at home, habitually enraging others with
superficial gentility that covered much more venomous sentiments.
For reasons yet unknown, I knew that Dana did not like doing what
others wanted of him.

> "Nice day, isn't it?" Dana added one last time in response to my
> noting that our time was up.
> I could have confronted Dana, saying something like, "Don't
> give me that sweet crap. You don't mean it's a nice day." Or,

perhaps, interpreting his behavior à la Hollywood, "You're just a little chicken. You're don't have the guts to do therapy. You don't have the balls to talk with me." Who would I been kidding? Such as outburst would have done nothing therapeutically good, serving mostly to vent my frustration.

"You know, it is a nice day," I replied, meaning it as I opened the door to see the sun shining, reminding myself that Dana's behavior, though aimed at me, was nothing personal about me.

Dana gave me a curious look, my temperance intriguing him. Although he didn't reply, he did come back the next week and the next for many months.

However unique the reasons for Dana's opposition to therapy, he wasn't the only child who sought to avoid therapy with me. I've met exquisitely anxious children for whom the prospect of meeting me, an unknown therapist, to address the very matters that frighten them was itself something very real and big to worry about. More than a few have barricaded themselves in their parents' car in the driveway of my office, refusing to come in. For one of those children our first four sessions consisted of my standing aside the car, talking through the small crack of the electric window that he controlled while burrowed on the floor under the dashboard. Only after I'd sufficiently demonstrated my patience and respect for his fear and need to control the situation did he dare venture into the office proper.

More frequently, the children who try to reject therapy from the onset are not anxious enough. These are children, mostly boys, who've been referred because of conflicts with the outside world at home and school. I save my words of how therapy can help them to better understand themselves or live a more fulfilled life. Mistrustful of any authority, they know the score: they've been dragged to me, not for self-realization, but to fix their badness. Why would any child feel good about seeing a man they assumed to be one more arm of the law, a co-conspirator who would use his therapeutic disguise to punish and change him?

In some cases my taking an interest in *their* side of the story gets us past their initial guard. Occasionally it does not. In such instances parents often need help and guidance in setting limits on their child's not coming, in finding ways that are firm and effective but do not involve physical aggression or abuse. That some of these homes have been characterized by wrongful uses of force alerts us to be wary, for some parents, if they think we approve, will hog-tie their children to our office. A child who is thrown into our office by the scruff of his neck is rather unlikely to feel good about us.

Yet occasionally there are children who require behavioral consequences for their lack of cooperation with therapy. These children, from overly lenient homes and headed for delinquency, need discipline and treatment. "Remove the computer from the home until they cooperate with therapy," I've recommended. "Take away their bicycle [or something else that means a lot to them]."

Although children initially detest this idea and its creator (a.k.a. me), they tend to respond well, apparently appreciating at some level that my intervention is in their best interest (because they need discipline and they need treatment) and is a sign of the desperate state their life is in. Once the child is captive in my office, inviting him to openly debate and criticize my opinion helps us to connect and quickly surmount whatever bad feeling was generated by my suggestion. Then, and only then, can I start to convince children that I am there primarily for them and their needs, however mandated their therapy is. "Any changes you make," I stress, "you'll make because you want to, not because I or anyone else is making you."

Many children balk at or become averse to therapy as it represents a narcissistic injury. The implication that they may need help offends them, particularly those who most need it. The children who are brought to our door may have been told that they are ill, sick, losers, disturbed, potential serial killers, or have broken brains (which is why we want to know what the child was told about therapy and ourselves and why they are coming). Even in the majority of cases

where the words were subtler, gentler, and more tactful, children read
their coming to a mental health professional as announcing their
defectiveness or abnormality, and signaling their being less than their
peers or what they or their parents want them to be.

When children tell us, "I don't need your help," they may
believe precisely the opposite. But even an awareness of their own
situation or stresses may not translate into motivation to get help.
Our telling them that they indeed do need us generally does little
more than make the child feel even smaller and more threatened.
These children appreciate our asking them how they figure they've
gotten to our doorstep.

> "My asshole father thinks I'm depressed," Geoff said with a disgusted
> look. "He's the depressed one. He's the one that should be seeing
> you. I don't need this."
>
> "He really needs to see someone?" I asked back, knowing that
> Geoff was right, knowing also that his dad actually was in treatment
> for depression with someone else.
>
> "He does sees someone," Geoff replied, showing me his
> honesty. "But it doesn't help him."
>
> "No?"
>
> "He walks around like he's going to kill himself any moment."
>
> "You worry about him," I noted, buoyed by Geoff's clear
> concern for his father, wondering how much his perceptions
> involved projections of his own suicidal thoughts. The boy's eyes
> watered.
>
> "I certainly don't know if you're depressed," I said. "You
> hardly know me and I hardly know you. But whatever the reasons
> your parents brought you here, you can make as much or as little
> of this as you wish."
>
> "Don't think I'm going to talk to you about my feelings and
> that crap."
>
> "You'll talk about what you want and nothing more."
>
> Geoff proceeded slowly, but gradually he did talk about what
> he wanted to: what it was like growing up with a father who was
> so preoccupied with suspicious fears of the world.

I specifically chose to highlight a case in which a boy's reluctance fell by the wayside rather easily and promptly. The majority of children who initially oppose me and the process can be reached with a modest amount of tolerance and the demonstration that I will follow them where they wish to go. I know from experience that a more authoritarian stance, or psychological speculation about the reasons for their fears (even just calling their disinclination toward therapy a fear), can lead them to dig their heels in deeper, if not to flee.

Other children benefit by our demonstrating that we see their wish not to come. We deliberately make statements that include a caboose of a phrase that at least implies their possibly, maybe, once in a while, having an issue that bothers them. "The last thing you want is some therapist poking around your business." "You want to manage your own affairs." "You believe in handling your own troubles." Children who are allergic to receiving help don't want to hear how we will give it to them in some special way. By letting them know that we know they don't want our help we show them we listen, meet them where they are, confirm and accept their feelings, and testify that our esteem can withstand being unwanted. It also shows children firsthand what therapy is like, how what we offer may be nothing like what they imagine we offer and which repels them.

Part of a child's rejection of therapy may reflect mistrust. This suspicion may be well founded following life experiences in which a child had been abused, neglected, or somehow mistreated by a parent or caregiver. As child therapists, we take great care to create an environment and structure that will allay such a child's worries. We willingly keep our doors open (so he can feel in contact with a trusted adult or simply the outside world), conduct therapy with the parent present if the child desires, show him how our doorknobs and locks work (making clear that he can control the comings and goings in the room), and give his need for personal space and safety wide berth. To children our proclamations of our trustwor-

thiness mean little and can feel dangerous, whereas our announce-
ment of our understanding for their caution ("After all, you know
nothing about me except that I'm a therapist") and support for their
getting to know us slowly does much to allay their protective reservations concerning therapy and us.

Children who have grown up in more sociopathic homes may
distrust our motives. They may think that therapists are self-serving. They assume we do our work solely for love of money and
have no true caring for them or their families. Our statements that
we do care about them and their welfare fall on deaf ears for they
have learned such claims are the manipulating tongue of con men.
They may ask questions that test us severely but that we can't afford to duck. "If you care so much about me, why don't you see
me for free?" Although to answer "Of course I would" may feel
good to us, it's probably not true and risks confirming the hunch
that we are liars. Our being straight with them and exhibiting our
caring over time is the only antidote to their cynicism.

The dependency of therapy can make children uncomfortable
and lead them to withhold their attachment and investment in treatment and the therapist. Essentially dreading saying goodbye, they
can never bring themselves to say hello. An unfair irony tends to
rule in this matter. Those whose dependency needs are strongest
commonly push others away the hardest, including the child therapist. These children, self-declared islands, find the nurturing shel-
ters we create seductive but perilous. They know, even in their short
lives, that others can't be counted on to be there, not die, not neglect,
not abuse, not abandon. Only fools, they are sure, grow reliant on
others. Such children may be hardened and cold-shouldered to
humanity or may have turned wholly to peers for the support
and affiliation they crave. We make contact with these children
slowly.

Passed among a chaotic and dysfunctional extended family because
no one, including his parents, had the resources to care for him

adequately and consistently, 9-year-old Vincent had come to depend on his own wits to get by. The social agency that managed his case had referred him to me for escalating aggression at school.

Vincent needed nobody. He told me so often in our beginning work. "No thanks," he said, politely declining my offer for a snack. He readily deflected my questions concerning his comfort (e.g., wanting more heat or fresh air). "Whatever you want," he'd reply. He was perfectly polite and willing to discuss whatever I brought up, but I felt as though I was an annoying fly that Vincent calmly brushed off again and again. (In fact, I'd seen Vincent deal with a bee in the office exactly that way, showing that he could care less about the insect, even as he chased it away.) "I have no needs," every word and gesture seemed to protest. "I'm okay with what I've got."

Several weeks into our meetings Vincent arrived with a bad cold. The dryness of the office caused him to cough. "Can I get you some water?" I asked, watching his clear discomfort. He held up his hand to signal no while struggling with a coughing jag that wouldn't end. Putting his physical need above the psychological one not to need, I brought him out a tall glass of water with a handful of hard candies. Still gagging, he took the water while holding up his hand to ward off the candy. A couple of sips did the trick and, the water barely touched, Vincent promptly put the glass on the table alongside the candy and thanked me. "It's awfully dry in here," I said, wanting to put the responsibility of his need on the environment (as if to say, "It's not your fault you needed water in here" and, going one step further, "it's not your fault you have needs"). Trivial as this act of giving and taking may seem, Vincent reacted severely. He grew more defiant at school—he'd settled down a bit since treatment—and withdrew even more in therapy, discussing neither his rejuvenated problems nor anything else.

The therapy barely thumped along until one day Vincent came to a session soaked from a thunderstorm. (Dressing for the weather would be admitting his needs to himself.) I offered to get him a towel.

"Fuck you!" he responded, cursing at me for the first time. Vincent looked away. I tried inquiring what might be bothering him: school, home, friends. But my words didn't touch him. I was stymied. Watching him dry his drenched head with a small piece of tissue he had, however, brought the light to me.

"You never asked for that water, did you?" I asked.

"What!" Vincent snapped, though I was certain he'd heard me.

"You never asked that for that water, did you?"

"I didn't ask for it and I didn't need it."

"I just brought it, didn't I?"

"I don't need any fucking thing from you. Or anybody else." Vincent's eyes reddened. We spent the remainder of the hour in silence.

Although he had a much better week at school following that hour, and soon after spontaneously asked me where those hard candies had gone, Vincent's fear of depending on me and people, while shrinking considerably, dogged every last inch of his therapy.

Needing not to need me, Vincent kept me at bay. A child's begrudging attitude, expressed notably in terms of criticism of the therapist, however, can carry meaning beyond that of fearing dependency.

Karin couldn't get along with anyone. She alienated her family, teachers, and peers. "He doesn't help me," she declared loudly, even in the initial hour, lobbying her parents to be excused from treatment. "I'm never going to talk with him," she promised them, though her wish to put me down moved her to speak continually. "You're stupid," she told me minutes later. She also informed me that I was ugly, boring, pathetic, queer, dishonest, and a complete waste of space.

Karin's name-calling didn't bother me, for it was easy to feel her presence and caring. But the tirades gradually faded and Karin spent more of each hour in quietude, with eyes closed and arms crossed, determined not to share any work with me. "He does me no good," she'd announce at the hour's end. "I don't even talk in there." Fortunately, her parents, feeling so at their rope's end, had no intention of stopping therapy however much she complained.

"It's perplexing," I said, during Karin's silence. "Your life's in a shambles. You're here anyway. And yet you stubbornly refuse to give it a try."

"For what?" Karin angrily came back. "I've been coming for two months and you haven't helped me yet."

"You haven't tried."

"I've come for weeks and my life's as screwed up as it ever was. You can't help me. No one can."

Karin's need to devalue me and therapy came, I soon learned, from her sense of utter hopelessness that no one could ever help her and make her life any different, any better. Establishing this despair together allowed the therapy to begin in earnest.

In most cases our child patients' reluctances in treatment reflect resistances that involve the therapeutic work itself, rather than the therapist's failure to engage them. Their misgivings are not aimed at us personally; that is, they are not resisting us as individuals. They resist looking at themselves honestly, out of fear of what they might see. For example, one boy preferred blaming his not skiing on his mother's overprotectiveness rather than acknowledging his own fear of injury and loss of control. None of us, including our child patients, wish to see parts of ourselves that tarnish our ideal images of who we are and who we want to become.

The benefit of clear self-vision, stressed throughout this book and continually demonstrated in our clinical work, is easier to grasp for some children. Consider a child whose bad-boy cruelty hides a strong underlying wish to be a good and caring child. Who would argue that his coming to see, accept, and take pride in that part of himself is anything but wonderful? What other children see in the mirror, however, may be less appreciated by families or society.

Mae was the sweetest of daughters. This 10-year-old was generous, nurturing, and considerate to a fault. An honors student and always the first to help out, she was every teacher's favorite. When others fought, she made peace. If it were not for the severe headaches and stomach pains for which she was referred, her life, her parents reported, would be perfect.

For many hours in therapy Mae showed herself to be the model citizen I'd been told about, concerned only for others' welfare, taking care of my office and me as much as she could. During one migraine attack, however, she expressed a smidgen of frustration over the noise of children in the waiting room. I was watching to see if that small venting of hostility might alleviate her headache, but it only worsened it. "I'm sorry," she said, near tears. "I'm just not feeling well."

"They are noisy, aren't they?" I concurred. "It could give anyone a headache, don't you think?" Now her face relaxed and a smile broke out. My tolerance and the sharing of her plaint comforted her and eased her pain.

Over her course of treatment Mae grew much more able to disagree and protest. As she became more open to making claims for her own needs, she was no longer the perfect little lady. While pleased that her bodily pains subsided, her parents were more ambivalent about the daughter she was becoming. She now fought with her family, occasionally had tensions with her teachers, and was not nearly as selfless as she once was. They appreciated Mae's becoming a more confident person who could assert her ideas, and they highly valued her becoming more able to protect herself even if it meant hurting another's feelings. Her fortified independence toward them, however, was much harder for them to adapt to and occupied much of Mae's worry and work on her way to growing up.

Looking at oneself honestly can be starkly lonely and pained. One boy may not like admitting that he wants to be an only child, for that, in his good-boy's mind, would make him his little sister's murderer. One girl may not want to know how badly she wishes she was a boy, fearing its homosexual meanings and, even more, not wanting to feel the sad hopelessness of that never-to-come-true fantasy. Another child may not like discovering just how devoted he is to being angry with his mother, believing that to let it go would be to wholly pardon her. For many adolescent boys, their wish to be taken care of in therapy evokes terrifying homophobia. The reasons none of us want to look ourselves in the eye are complex, deep, and substantial.

While a child's resistance can manifest itself suddenly or in highly discrete moments, it much more often permeates the entire fabric of a therapy, rising and falling in different contexts and under varying stresses. This resistance does not avert unwanted insights per se as much as it wards off the demand for change that awareness brings. If a boy admits that he is selfish, he then bears the responsibility of staying selfish or of becoming more giving.

If I'm hostile, do I want to stop fighting and hurting people? If my insecurity leads me to put down other children, am I willing to treat them better? If I am afraid of everything, am I willing to take risks to master my worry? Whatever the precise form of a child's resistance, it almost always involves some variation on the wish to never grow up. That is why the lag between significant insights and behavioral changes can be great and discouraging—to the child, his parents, and the therapist. General resistance to the losses and responsibilities of growing up is at the core, I have found, of almost every child's treatment.

As we know too well, parents' resistance is an equally likely obstacle to our work with their child.

> Mrs. Newman loved her son dearly. She a single mother and he an only child, they enjoyed, for better and worse, an embattled, enmeshed, and overly intimate relationship. Having brought Harry in with a growing depression, she felt much genuine appreciation that therapy was working. Which is why I was caught off guard by her last-minute canceling of three sessions in a month's period. "He's sick," "I'm sick," and "He has too much schoolwork to get done for tomorrow" were the messages she left (contrasting with her typically friendly and expansive style).
>
> "Sick?" Harry asked, when I asked about his health on his return. Harry explained that he'd missed sessions because his mother: took him to buy a bicycle in lieu of coming to the first missed session;

took him to a movie instead of his second; and invited him to skip school the morning of the third with the provision that he not leave the house all day.

I didn't have to hit Mrs. Newman on the head with my finding that she'd lied. To do so would have humiliated her, put Harry in an impossible place, and thrown the therapy off track. Instead, I shared with Mrs. Newman my realization of how hard it can be to bring a child to a therapist.

This simple statement of empathy tapped a torrent of emotions: fear that I would steal her son away, dread that I was the parent she wished she could have been, jealousy that her son's treatment was working better than her own, and a pained conviction that she caused him hurt (i.e., depression) but that I healed him. "Do you know what it's like to feel like you have to bribe your own child with gifts to make him like you more?" she asked, in all of the anguish a parent can feel, confessing and interpreting in that awful question all that she'd done the past month. Mrs. Newman and I made a deal that day, which she kept, that should she feel that I was growing too close to her son, she would take me to task (with words) rather than act on that impulse.

Most parents feel bad that their child is suffering or having sufficient troubles to need our services. Few parents celebrate their child's coming for treatment. The changes that the child makes may force changes at home; such disequilibriums in the family as a whole are at the heart of family-systems–based treatments. The child's being in therapy, and the matters that inevitably arise, confront parents with hard reality that may clash with their ideals of the parents they wanted to be and the dreams they held for their children. Beyond the obvious narcissistic injury, these realizations can cause profound heartache and despair.

As underlined in the previous chapter on parent work, we must always keep watch for signs of such resistance. We try to avert the growth of these doubts to lethal proportions, lest parents pull the plug on the treatment. We encourage them, making clear their obligation, to share their frustrations with us and the effects of therapy. We don't let too many no-shows or last-minute cancellations pass before trying to understand them and do something constructive. Rather than defensively justify the costs and effort of therapy, we try to understand the sacrifice parents are making as well as the resentment that can follow. We also consider the possible red herrings their protests may pose as we listen for the more basic ambivalence toward therapy that may underlie them.

THERAPEUTIC CRISES

We all know a crisis when we see one: a person stands on the edge of a bridge, or threatens someone with a steak knife, or violently assaults another, or swallows a bottle of medication. I leave the discussion of those horrors to another book, another author. In this section I discuss what I call *therapeutic crises*, meaning junctures or phases in a sound and ongoing therapy where there is: deterioration of symptoms, behaviors, or functioning; a disturbing lack of progress; heightened (or newly surfaced) self-destructive impulses; or a serious narcissistic blow to our child patients or their parents.

I looked at the family before me. Mr. and Mrs. Isley appeared as deeply stressed as their son, Leo, who'd been in treatment with me for the past year and a half. Although Leo's anxiety and timidity had diminished dramatically during the first eleven months, he'd gone downhill since. His school, which had cheered his blossoming, was calling again with concerns over just how tense and unable to function this fifth-grader was. "What can we do?" the parents asked, just as they'd asked so many times before.

Following a sudden profit in the stock market a couple of years earlier the Isleys had bought a massive estate along the riverfront. Although Mr. Isley had no regular job or income, that windfall had convinced him of future good fortune and attested to his giftedness as an investor. But the times had turned down fast. Greed and impulsivity had led Mr. Isley to make several bad decisions that cost them most of their savings. Facing the possibility of bankruptcy, Mr. Isley had begun drinking (an old problem for him), as had Mrs. Isley.

When we met they discussed the overwhelming stress that their mortgage payment was having on them. "If we just sold the estate," they explained repeatedly, "we could buy an extremely nice home and have a good deal of savings. Less stressed we could function better, find ourselves jobs." They looked at Leo. "And we know this is killing the kids."

I nodded my head in agreement.

Although I proceeded to make clear my opinion that the stress was killing all of them, and that the resurgence of alcoholism would only complicate matters, I was handcuffed. They understood the impact their financial situation was having on themselves and their family, yet losing that property and all that it meant was almost impossible for them.

Tempted to give up, I continued. The fact that the Isleys continued to come signaled at least some ambivalence, and I stayed true to my child patient. Leo still needed my help to stay afloat in this overwrought family, but eventually found himself able to confront his parents on their selfishness and how it was destroying him. It was his doing so that moved them to take the action that was long overdue, which did bring them much of the relief and hope they'd imagined.

There have been other families, however, whom I have been unable to reach in this way, and from whom I actually resigned.

"I know it's the weekend but I'm really afraid for Kent."

Hearing this message I called Mrs. Thiessen. She described how 8-year-old Kent had stolen again. We scheduled an appointment for Sunday morning.

Mrs. Thiessen told me how Kent had stolen a pocketbook from his neighbor. I was bothered by the fact that he'd deliberately planned the crime on the day this kindly widow, a woman who was good to him, cashed her Social Security check. But I wasn't shocked: this young child from an affluent home had stolen many times before. He lied habitually and blamed others. His character, sad to say, was quite flawed.

For at least the third time we discussed a fitting punishment. Mr. and Mrs. Thiessen thought their disapproval should be sufficient even though this was becoming a repetitive problem. I suggested that Kent be made to work for two hours each afternoon for fifty cents an hour until he'd earned back all of the money plus interest. The parents, worried about his becoming a sociopath, agreed enthusiastically.

Several weeks later, however, I received another frantic call: Kent had stolen again. While sharing their upset about this new incident, the parents made clear their displeasure with my inquiring about the previous one. "How was that discipline going?" I asked, having received a note from them that "it seemed to be having an effect" on Kent. With some prodding I learned that Kent had done no work. "We just don't have any work that a child can do at our house," Mr. Thiessen declared. "And besides, what do you expect me to do? Stand there for an hour a day watching to make sure Kent works?"

To make a long story short I eventually resigned from the case—one of only two such terminations—making it clear that I could not help Kent, that talking with me would bring him no benefit as long as his dishonest and scheming behavior was minimized and tolerated. Neither willing to do what was needed nor willing to examine their reasons for that apathy, the play and talking cure was wholly useless.

One of the commonest therapeutic crises is when old symptoms recirculate, coming back with a vengeance.

Andy's parents had brought her to therapy because of her uncontrollable tantrums. But over the past year she'd grown much in her capacity to tolerate frustration and to accept limitations. The birth of a new sister, however, brought her tantrums back with explosive force. "We can't take her anymore," her mother tearfully confessed.

My helping Andy's mother remember the gains her daughter had made, while confirming her frustration (particularly her being overwhelmed by new motherhood), steadied the home front a bit. My putting Andy's regression into a developmental context, predicting its passage, was enough to settle Andy's mother, who feared not so much today's or tomorrow's tantrum, but that her difficulties would go on if not escalate forever.

Parents' impulsive decisions to stop therapy can often indicate a crisis, as it did with Austin.

"This is Mrs. Bates. Austin won't be coming for therapy anymore. Thanks for all your help. Just send us the last bill and we'll pay you immediately."

Mrs. Bates had never felt close to me, but her unexpected message was even colder than I'd considered her to be. Given how beautifully her 12-year-old son, Austin, had done in therapy—brought because of pervasive inhibition due to a dog phobia that followed his having been bitten—her bulletin frankly shocked me. I wondered what I might have said or done to offend her, but couldn't come up with anything.

I waited a few days, hoping that whatever was burning might have cooled, and called her. She didn't want to talk, but when I expressed fear that I'd somehow let *her* down, she opened up. Mrs. Bates told me with fury how, when she entered the bathroom during her son's bath, Austin had pushed her out, telling her he wanted privacy. The kicker was when he told her that he hated her.

"But he's doing much better now, isn't he?" I said naively.

"I don't care how he's doing. I'd rather have him depressed. I'm not going to tolerate any son of mine saying that he hates me."

I was horrified that a mother could say that about her own child. But I reminded myself, "Wasn't it she who brought him to therapy?" Besides, it hit me, hadn't therapy taken off, not when he played out dog attacks, but when he connected his fear of dogs and his fear of his mother, a woman who could be cruelly intimidating? Supervising myself, I responded more suitably. "You bring your son for therapy and what do you get for it?" I asked Mrs. Bates, hoping she'd let me back in.

And she did. For Mrs. Bates, like any mother who loves her son, didn't want to be hated by him. While I saw Austin's hatred as expressing the other side of his deep love, an expression that would make room for them to grow even closer, she heard only hatred that in her worst nightmares would grow and grow until he'd want nothing to do with her ever. Yet more than many mothers, Mrs. Bates had some sense that how she'd treated her son had given him good reason to hate her.

When parents threaten the end of therapy, we must take their thinking seriously. What might be triggering their upset, we ask ourselves? Our own retaliative and impulsive urge to find out fast, to alleviate our own worries (that it isn't something we'd done), or to convince them otherwise is paradoxically the longest way around. Slow and steady is the course, leaving much room for parents and ourselves to wallow in and come to better know what good reasons are making them doubt whether therapy is in their child's best interest. Almost without exception, parents' abrupt decisions to terminate therapy signal that something important is afoot, something that must be tracked down and reckoned with, not just to renew the therapy but to resolve a matter that likely holds significance for the child and parent as well as the treatment.

Perhaps the most difficult of therapeutic crises is when a child expresses a wish to die. This wish may make itself known in a passing bedtime utterance, "I wonder what the point of living is?" It can come more dramatically, during a frustrated homework moment: "I hate myself. I'm so stupid. I wish I'd just die." Or be observed in endless sobbing, accompanied by hopelessness, helplessness, and sometimes cruel self-deprecating. Such distress is never easy to see or hear. For a loving parent to hear a child wish himself dead is beyond painful.

"Rock can't stop crying," his mother, who'd asked for this hour, told me with her own wet eyes. She held her head in her hands.

"What is it?" I asked

"What did I do," she asked herself in my presence, barely able to get the words out, "to make my baby hate himself?"

I sat and said nothing, allowing Rock's mother to cry all she needed. She didn't need me to answer this question, to give her a laundry list of parenting faults and missteps. Nor did I rush to undo the guilt she felt. My job was to stay with her in this awful place she found herself.

At the hour's end I explained what I knew for sure. Rock had been doing better than ever. Once thoroughly depressed and dysfunctional, he was living life. He had become an active and successful member of his classroom. He'd made a couple of friends even if he still hung back socially. Depressive bodily symptoms had improved: eating again, he'd gained twelve pounds; he could fall asleep in less than an hour versus the several he used to require; and he had become a somewhat avid bike rider.

Once much too depressed and forlorn to discuss his obvious suffering—including the traumatic loss of a father who, when rock was 4, had left town and his son for good—Rock had grown strong enough to feel his hurt and to share it. "Rock," I explained, "is feeling good enough to finally withstand that sadness."

"You mean his crying is a good thing?" his mother asked with hope in her eyes.

I readily nodded my affirmation, knowing that what she'd said was exactly the way it was.

In a majority of cases, when child patients who are firmly ensconced in therapy with me talk of death and hating themselves, I find myself encouraged, sometimes elated. For months, usually years, these children have, all alone, carried their horrid sense that they are bad, sick, evil, crazy, or worse. The boy who can finally tell his parents and his therapist of these sentiments has come a long way in trust, resiliency, and hope. He feels good enough about himself to think that another person will care about his hurt. He feels optimistic enough to believe that sharing his hurt will bring some relief or consolation. He's come to recognize that shedding these weighty thoughts can bring a lightness not known before. Ironically, his sharing these thoughts generally means that he is not so persuaded that he is in fact as disturbed, insane, or worthless as he once judged himself to be.

While scary thoughts can lead us to fear for the child's welfare, we may also worry about legal matters and our liability. It is imperative that we try to keep those needs distinct from what transpires and is warranted clinically. Hospitals occasionally can keep children safe, but in general not much happens therapeutically. Children are typically released in much the same state as they were admitted, ready now to begin the outpatient therapy that has been unnecessarily delayed.

Of course, children who are in danger, who are trying to kill themselves or hurt others, need to be protected. However, when a child is working steadily in a productive therapeutic relationship, verbal expressions of self-hatred and suicide and even milder acts of self-destruction can often be best left in the trusting, hopeful, and holding hands we offer them.

We, as therapists, firmly hold our child patients and their parents through this necessary misery on the road to recovery and healing. But we can only do so when we truly believe that what we are seeing is a good sign. We strive at these trying times to see clearly the context of the child's life and therapy. Fitful crying jags or suicidal ideation in themselves say little about the prognosis or how serious things are. I have yet to see any serious therapy, with child or adult, not come to moments of existential doubt. To live a thinking life is, I believe, to have times of utter despair and questions as to the purpose and value of life. The more closely and carefully we follow children and their therapy from the initial steps across our threshold, the more likely we are to understand and know how to handle the inevitable crises that evolve in the course of this tumultuous work.

Even the most skilled and successful of therapies is prone to obstacles, detours, and crises. These seeming impasses need not be signs of the patient's deterioration or the therapist's negligence (though they can be, of course). To the contrary, in a well-founded treatment relationship they often speak to points of opportunity that, if appreciated in their unique context, can richly facilitate a therapy and bring greater understanding, not just to those patients, but to all of our clinical work.

13

WHEN THERAPY
IS NOT ENOUGH:
MEDICATION

As the biologizing of the mind has grown more widespread, more and more attention has been focused on the developing of drugs to treat most every troubling symptom and behavior. Like most advances in science, this virtual explosion of psychotropic medication has both solved and created problems. It has been a godsend to many, while it has harmed others and done not much for the rest. This chapter examines the role of medicine and its implications for children and their therapies.

Perhaps the primary question when we first meet a child is whether he or she seems to warrant medication. The history that we collect in our evaluation gives us some perspective, though our richest data is from our observations of the child. We ask ourselves whether he is unduly hurting. In assessing him, his and his parents' self-awareness, sensitivity, and sense of drama all need to be taken seriously. Does the child exaggerate her upset, and if so, for what and whose benefit? There are children, too, who minimize their pain, who walk around for months silently bearing the psychic equivalent of a broken leg. Are parents accurately sensing their child's ordeal? Do they blow his minor frustrations out of proportion or conversely do they not take his suicidally tinged self-disparaging seriously? Emotional pain is subjective and can't easily be measured as one might check the child's red blood cell count.

Likewise, what do we make of children who exhibit behaviors that cause themselves and others problems and grief but that they claim they cannot control? How do we know what their effort has been? Will our work with them, we wonder, be the key to triggering greater self-control? We wallow through the morass, wanting neither to push for unnecessary medication nor to deny medical treatment that might bring a child deserved relief and behavioral benefit.

> Nine-year-old Toby appeared as depressed as his parents and teacher had described him. He sat perfectly still in his chair, answering my questions with flat and telegraphically short responses, and showing no interest in my toys or me. When I asked, Toby's parents stressed that, however unmistakably sullen, Toby never talked of being sad, of not liking himself, or of wanting to die. "If not for his constant moping about," his mother said with unrecognized irony, "we'd never know anything is wrong with him."
>
> Toby's parents, with the school's endorsement, were hoping that I in this first hour—despite their knowing that I was a psychologist—might give Toby a prescription for an antidepressant. "We can't stand seeing him like this anymore," his father said.
>
> But depressed as he appeared, I refrained. Toby, in reply to my last-minute query about whether he was as miserable as his parents told me and as he appeared, showed a bit of life. "I hate my parents. I hate myself. And there's nothing anyone or any medicine can do to make me feel any better."
>
> Toby's sudden determination told me much. He had feelings, strong ones, even if they were slow to come out. His passivity and gloominess involved unexpressed hostility. Toby was not happy with his life as it was; his proclaiming his helplessness said to me that he wanted help, if only it could be found. His final assertion that no person or drug could help also seemed to ring of some resentment

and opposition to his being brought here and to his obvious knowledge of his parents' wish that he be medicated. His parting remark—"You won't tell my parents what I said, will you?"—attested, I thought, to his conflict with and caring for his parents as well as some connecting with me as his therapist.

Buoyed by what I saw in Toby, and hearing how his parents' frustration stoked their desire that he be medicated (i.e., fixed fast), I comfortably put off a medical consultation. "Let's give therapy a chance first," I suggested, "and we'll give drugs a look at the first sign that they're needed."

They never were.

When children are brought to us with internal distress, primarily depression, anxiety, or some admixture—and they have had no previous therapy—it may be best to delay medication and give the therapy a month or so to get on sure footing. To begin medication and therapy at the same time can be confusing. The child must somehow work out a relationship with two clinicians. Most critically, beginning therapy and a new medication together makes for bad science, for confounded experiments. If the child shows relief, how do we know whether to credit the medicine or the therapy? Should the child show seeming side effects, how can we be sure they are not born of stress due to a new treatment? While such questions are seldom crystal clear, adding two variables at once is likely to cloud our thinking about the child. In a majority of cases medication can judiciously be stalled to allow therapy to get established, thereby providing a more solid foundation for drugs should they prove to be needed.

Our slowing down the request for medications is often comforting. Parents who've suffered alongside their children for some time may be desperate for help. Our steady welcome and holding, letting them know of our concerned awareness for their child's symptoms and affirming that we are keeping the question of medication on the front burner to be closely watched, generally calms their worry. I've found child patients just as open to my suggestion that we contemplate medication more carefully only after we've had a chance to get to know each other and to get to see how helpful my work with them can be.

The child who is referred because of impulsivity, distractibility, hyperactivity, and misbehavior presents a slightly different problem. The job of teasing out depression from worry from neurological issues from environment can be tedious and time consuming. Such children typically have neither an interest in nor tolerance for discussing their feelings; they often have no wish for therapy. These children, particularly if they have had less-than-successful trials of treatment previously, may be clearer candidates for medication. I have tended to err in the opposite direction, being a conservative in terms of medication, waiting too long to recommend drugs that can help a distracted child learn better or be less frenetic at home. Because medication might be a catalyzing factor in therapy with these children, it might well be initiated sooner rather than later in a treatment.

When the therapy proceeds well enough to support its continuing, but fails to bring needed relief soon enough, and nothing in the process leads us to believe that great improvement is just around the corner, it may be time to obtain that pharmacological consultation. Before calling for an evaluation, however, we may benefit by discussing the matter with the child for whom medication is being considered. Talking with children about the severity of their distress, the frustration of their distractibility, and the depths of their pessimism lays the groundwork to explore the possibility of medical intervention.

Care must be taken here to put the notion of medicine into the context of the therapy. A simplistic "therapy isn't working so we better try drugs" will likely make the child feel a failure and exacerbate whatever distress exists. In fact, if a question remains about whether the therapy or we as therapists are helping that child, we need to broach that topic first and separately. A child should never be sent for medicine to avert our own frustrations over a lack of clinical progress or understanding.

Some children are open to medicine. They like the idea of a pill that can make life look less dark or reduce their panic. Some are ambivalent, wondering if a drug could really help, but wary of its side effects or potential for addictiveness. Others, often those most needing it, are vehemently opposed, phobically fearing that it might poison them or change their personalities. Hypervigilant to any intrusion into their body or mind, they see drugs as devil stuff meant to control them as the mistrusted authorities in their world see fit. More than a few children, children who suffer horrendous self-hatred, feel themselves undeserving of a medicine that might lift their guilt and depression, making them happier.

Taking a week or two (or many more) to help a child work through his feelings about medication is always time well spent. A child who holds a cooperative attitude toward medication will provide the consulting psychiatrist with the most reliable and useful data, resulting in the best-informed prescription and optimum compliance. A child who is dragged to the psychiatrist, sometimes unavoidably, will be apt to fight the interview as well as resist the medicine once at home. As a rule, whatever useful exploring a child does around the issue of medication holds more generalizable value for his therapy and self-examination as a whole.

It is ideal when we can refer to psychiatrists with whom we can communicate and who have an understanding for the kind of therapy we do. Most psychiatrists, however busy, appreciate the therapist's observations with reference to the child's symptoms, function, response to the therapeutic relationship, and feelings toward medication. Their job—assessing and prescribing for dozens of children whom they see for limited periods of time—gets tougher every day, making them ever more amenable to whatever information or thoughts we can offer. Although they tend to know the medicines best, we've had the luxury of knowing our patients in ways they cannot. We also can provide these overworked clinicians with an ear to bounce their thinking off. A five-minute phone call may be just enough to prompt the prescriber to rethink the deci-

sion to prescribe yet a fifth drug or add another medication during
the same week the child is entering a new classroom. It's always
fascinating, too, to hear of the material the consulting psychiatrist
often garners when meeting our patients, revelations (particularly
about symptoms) that have somehow passed under our eyes or over
our heads or that the child chose not to share with us.

In the course of deeper and more tumultuous therapies it is
not rare for the child to undergo anguished phases where troubling
behaviors or unsettling symptoms reappear with a fury. These therapeutic crises can scare the child, her parents, and the therapist, discouraging everyone along the way. The utmost care needs to be
taken to judge what is transpiring. Rushing reflexively to medication risks undermining the hard work that is progressing and giving
children the impression that their darkest and ugliest innards cannot be borne by those they depend on (their parents, their therapist). Confused and thrown as these therapeutic upheavals can make
us, the child needs us to hold tight, to resist such pressures as the
fear of legal repercussions, public opinion, and school disapproval
that can propel us toward unnecessary action that may sabotage the
therapy and waste the therapeutic opportunity of the crisis.

Twelve-year-old Steven was a nervous wreck. His rigid body
resembled a robot's and his tense face showed no emotion but dread.
He'd been referred for high anxiety, obsessions of being harmed, a
compulsive need to wash his hands and play with numbers, and
constant frustration. Apprehensive of infectious disease and the
dangers of intimacy, he'd withdrawn from peers and could barely
function in the child- and germ-filled atmosphere of the school.

Steven made great progress during the first year of treatment.
Over countless sessions full of primitive explosions and panicked
shows of shame and repentance, Steven grew much more accepting
of his enraged jealousy of a deaf brother who got most of his parents'
attention. Although he stopped doting on his brother, the boys grew
closer and more compatible. His compulsions all but disappeared and
he became a welcome, if a bit shy, member of the sixth-grade culture.

These wondrous gains made his sudden disintegration that much more disconcerting. Within a week's time Steven appeared to lose all his hard-won progress. He refused to eat, fearing his food was tainted by his mother's hands. Cruelty absolutely ruled his treatment of his brother, leading Steven, a bright boy, to learn curses and other phrases in sign language to put his brother down. He withdrew entirely in school, breaking down into crying jags that required him to leave the class. Most disturbing of all, he took to punching his own head and twisting his fingers so hard that he'd bruise his knuckles. I learned all this on one day via frantic calls from the school principal, his guidance counselor, his parents, and even Steven himself, who asked to see me a day early.

In that hour Steven could do no more than cry and repeatedly say that he had no idea what was happening to him. "Maybe I'm going crazy," was all he could come up with. For several weeks I received frantic calls from school and home, at first encouraging me to get Steven some medication, eventually questioning what I was doing with the boy.

Fending off my own self-doubt, I reread session notes and thought hard about all that had happened over the past thirteen months. I worried about his disintegrating. "Should I be taking swifter action?" I kept asking myself. Yet I was certain there was some good reason for this regression, and feared doing anything that might throw a wrench into what might be a therapeutic opening as much as it was a challenge.

It wasn't until the third week of doubled sessions that we hit pay dirt. Passing my children's bicycles in the driveway, Steven remembered dreaming that his brother had been run down by a train. "He was riding like mad to catch up with me. He didn't hear the train or the signal." Steven began to punch the chair.

"He didn't really die," I said.

"But," Steven said, his chest heaving with emotion, his fists whacking the side of his head. "I wanted him to." Steven punched himself again. "I wanted him to die." Steven fell to the floor, wailing.

Late in the hour, relieved of his enormous hurt, Steven figured out that his dream had come the day after he'd tried to ditch his brother at the mall. Immediately feeling guilty, he'd raced back to get his brother only to see him running wildly through the mall looking for Steven. "He tripped over a trash can he was so upset," Steven recalled with a half cry, half laugh.

Although he required a good several weeks more of therapy to get back to where he'd been, Steven soon was growing even more quickly than before. We'd stayed the course together.

There are times, on the other hand, where child patients are reexperiencing a trauma or loss that it's clear will not resolve itself quickly. Although therapy is frequently arduous and painful, and despite the teachings as to religious salvation, inordinate suffering is neither a virtue nor necessarily healthful. A child's hurt, while often accompanying the working through of bad experiences and coming to terms with his limitations, need not be intolerable for growth and repair to proceed. In such cases I have referred my patients for short to moderate courses of medication to keep their distress to bearable levels. In none of the cases has the medication instantly made the child happy and carefree. The drugs merely dull the crippling anxieties and depression that have been tormenting a child beyond belief, enabling the therapeutic work to continue unabated.

While psychotropic medications have their place, some skepticism is warranted. Many medications have significant side effects. Some of these, such as the potential for heart damage with the tricyclics, require parents to make very difficult decisions. I've seen many parents tortured over this horrendous choice: watching their child's psychic pain but worried that their decision to okay a medicine will cause that loved one real physical harm. Sometimes no side effects more accurately translates into no discernible side effects thus far. That the mechanisms of many of these drugs are unknown, and that they act on the most basic parts of the brain (the physiological seat of the human heart and soul), should be enough to fuel our unrelenting caution toward psychiatric drugs.

We who see the child much more frequently than the prescribing clinician can help the child and family monitor as well as manage less life-threatening side effects. Highly suggestive or sensitive children often do best by not knowing all of the various adverse effects their medication can elicit. Ample discussion of the child's feelings about taking medicine—our job even more than that of the prescriber—can help to minimize untoward reactions. We also can help to confirm or assuage parents' anxieties about side effects they are unsure they are seeing, supporting contact with the child's psychiatrist when necessary. When we see that something is not quite right—strange motorisms with an antipsychotic—we can make sure that the prescribing clinician is notified.

Not only can premature or frivolous medicating interfere with treatment, but drugs that overly numb a child or cloud or slow her thinking can obstruct her functioning outside and inside therapy. I have seen Ritalin help many, but I've also seen it exacerbate underlying anxieties, causing obsessive children to obsess more. This rigidifying effect on feeling and thinking, besides feeling uncomfortable and strange, can deenergize a therapy, making children much less accessible to themselves and the freer aspects of self-exploration. Just as often, though, alleviating an overwhelming symptom does not defuse a child's motivation to do the hard work of therapy. Aptly administered drugs—antidepressants, for example—can do precisely the opposite, mobilizing a child who otherwise lacks the energy or hopefulness to engage in a treatment.

Particularly with the ADHD diagnosis, children need to understand the meaning of their taking drugs. Some are prone to interpret it as a straitjacket in tablet form. Parents, teachers, and therapists quick to attribute a good day to medicine or a bad day to its absence can unwittingly promote a child's abdication of personal responsibility. The drug is intended to help children organize and attend so they can have good experiences and feel successful. However, children often come to see the power that the adults in their lives attribute to that little pill. Ongoing discussion will monitor the child's feeling about the medicine and its effects, with the goal of raising the child's awareness of the effects of his own behavior and self-control.

Another major jeopardy of medication is that it can detour necessary or better intervention. Hopeful that a pill can fix their child's hurts and misbehavior (and who can blame them?), some parents are prone to shelve the more plodding work of therapy temporarily while they wait for an appointment at an ADHD clinic, for example, or for an antidepressant to reach therapeutic blood levels. Just as some prefer psychological explanations, others would rather hear that their child's difficulties are purely neurological or congenital and have little to do with anything that has gone on at the home. Therapists can counter this risk by supporting parents' interest in medication and robustly acknowledging the temperamental and biological bases of our beings, all the while making the limitations of drugs known and promoting the need to continue nonmedical efforts to improve the child's environment.

Unfortunately, the enthusiasm that greets new medications can go overboard. Psychology and psychiatry are as susceptible to the influence of fads as is the world of fashion and music. Diagnoses come and go with a fervor. Psychiatrists, especially those under the thumb of health care organizations and restraining insurance plans, are pushed to see more and more patients in less and less time. Wanting to help the suffering they see, knowing in many cases that the longer-term therapy that's needed is not an option, and increasingly beset by the demands of parents, they prescribe more medicine more easily. Although the official guidelines for prescribing most of these drugs are prudent, the majority of physicians, general psychiatrists, and child psychiatrists who prescribe them do not have the time or support to follow them. As the child's advocates, as the ones who may know his psychological needs best, child therapists help keep watch against quick-and-easy labeling or prescribing that does not take full enough account of who the child is.

Regardless of how hard we work and how skilled are the prescribing clinicians with whom we communicate so closely, there will be many cases that do not flourish. Psychotic and enraged children may need drug trial after drug trial, no one medication helping for more than a limited time. Children and parents may work for months to grow comfortable with the idea of medication only to discover that it brings no miracles. And, as we all know, there are parents who won't consider medication under any circumstances, however rough their child's problems and internal life.

Drugs deserve their rightful and major place in the treatment of children. Prescribed wisely and introduced thoughtfully into a child's therapy they can enormously facilitate a child's relief, functioning, and therapeutic growth. Administered carelessly or against a child's will, they can be useless or worse. Attending to the meanings medication holds for children, their parents, and their treatment can have everything to do with the success of the drug therapy, the play and talk therapy, and their integration.

14

ALL'S WELL THAT ENDS WELL: CLOSING THERAPY

All good things must come to an end, and that is just as true for therapy. Termination can follow a brief treatment or one that traverses much of a child's childhood. Planned or spontaneous, willing or forced, smooth or tumultuous, discouraging or encouraging, for good reason or bad, satisfying or much less so, termination can take many forms. This final chapter examines the simultaneously universal and varied ways in which children (and their parents) leave therapy as well as the equally common and diverse ways that we, their therapists, help or hinder their doing so.

To begin our look at endings, and prior to addressing the optimal criteria for proper endings, we must recognize that many therapies end for other than clinically good reasons.

> Owen's therapy had been having a positive effect. His violent temper and rabid defiance toward authority were both quieting. Even his mother, a most critical woman who'd put me through the third degree before letting me near her son, was looking pleased. But my refusal to shut her divorced husband out of Owen's therapy (and, as she tried, out of the boy's life), led her to end therapy abruptly

with no notice. Only at my insistence did she grudgingly give the boy and me a dozen or so minutes to say goodbye, a goodbye that consisted mostly of my confirming his dazed disbelief at his mother's unreasonableness. "This is awful," I said softly, with a minute left. Owen shook his head in sad agreement. "You can call me or write anytime," I added, doubting that he ever would. Owen left with his mother, knowing, it seemed, that he would never again see me.

In any suddenly aborted treatment, we do our best to acknowledge the traumatic ending, the value of our relationship, and the work that has been done, and offer any wisdom or strategies that might help the child cope without us. This applies, for example, to treatments that are increasingly being shut down by insurance companies or HMOs no longer willing to pay for them.

Felicia was a sweet child who'd put her dozen or so sessions to good use. Her palpable anxiety and school phobia had diminished, though she remained exquisitely vulnerable to the stresses of school and the slings and arrows of daily life. Having informed me that their insurance company's benefits had changed, allotting us one more session, her parents made clear that, even with the modest reduced fee I immediately offered, her therapy would be ending. "She's much better," they said. "We haven't gotten a call to pick her up from school in almost two months."

Wondering what other resistance played a role here, I tried my best to hear the parents' misgivings, hoping to incite their own judgment that, however well Felicia and her therapy had been doing, she needed more. Although I wanted to tell them all the bad things that might happen if Felicia was to quit, to frighten them into staying, I refrained. I knew that they could worry at least as well as I about their daughter's future. Moreover, sensing there was a likelihood that these parents were going to go off with Felicia, the last thing I wished to do was hang swords of bad prophecy over their heads to further strain their already stressed life.

Once it was eminently apparent that they had made up their minds, I bargained for one additional session, making them an offer (of a fee) they couldn't refuse. Having thus doubled the number of ending sessions available, I used one with Felicia, to close up her work with me. I devoted the all-important second one to her parents, to provide them some strategies to help Felicia cope without therapy as well as to have a bit more time to cultivate our alliance in hopes of further nurturing their nurturing of Felicia; I sought also to bid them adieu with as much connection and good feeling as possible so they would not be shy to return to me or another therapist should their daughter need help.

Tragically, I have twice seen parents close down their child's therapy because it was helping. In both cases a child was hated by its dutiful mother. Although the children had made great internal gains in their work with me, the weight of their mothers' unwavering and unquestioned dislike proved too heavy to oppose. The little time I had to end treatment with these children was spent in sad farewell, reminding them of their self-worth, ways in which I'd miss them, and, most important, ways to continue fending off their mother's hatred and to keep open to the good love they deserved, which others would give them.

Parents aren't the only ones to stop ongoing therapies in their tracks. The therapist in training, or who is changing jobs, frequently brings good therapies to an end well before their due time.

"You're full of shit." During his yearlong therapy Quentin had occasionally cursed in passing frustration, but he'd never aimed his swears at me. The 12-year-old looked down as he rolled a small toy car back and forth on my desk.

"What's the matter?" I asked, knowing that it was our terminating, but lost as to his accusation.

"I thought I could trust you."

He'd felt lied to or betrayed, I understood. But about what? Our ending? I'd given him fair warning at the start of our work that, as an intern, I'd be leaving the training site and his therapy come the last week of June (and that week was almost here). I knew he hadn't forgotten because he'd interrupted me to mention it when I first broke the news that we had only eight weeks of therapy left.

"Everyone else lies to me, but I thought you were different." Quentin's voice cracked with disappointment and hurt; there was no joke or showboating here.

Had I neglected to bring something I'd said I would? I didn't think so, but anything was possible.

"You act so sad about leaving me." Quentin continued, in a mockingly saccharine voice. "We worked so hard together." "I wish we didn't have to stop." "We only have eight weeks left."

"Those are my words," I said, impressed by the clarity of Quentin's listening and remembering.

"What bullshit," Quentin again accused. "Is someone putting a gun to your head?"

I tilted my head, unsure what he was asking.

"Is someone making you leave this building at gunpoint?" he asked.

"No."

"Is someone making you take that new job?"

I shook my head no.

"You'll be making more money there?"

I nodded that I would be.

"But you don't really want that job?" Quentin had dropped the car and was now walking about the office with the swagger of a prosecuting attorney, confident in his rightness. "You'd *really* rather stay here forever, making less money working with me? Isn't that right?"

I was at a loss for words. Quickly getting his message, I wanted to right the wrong I'd done. I wanted to answer honestly. But I didn't want to hurt his feelings. And besides, the answer wasn't that black and white. Yes, I wanted the new job, but I also would have liked to keep working with Quentin. But this boy—who in his confronting of me was showing me so much of the gains he'd made over the past year—rescued me with yet another question.

"Why couldn't you just say the truth? Quentin," he said, becoming me, "we've done a lot of good work together, and I'm going to miss you. But I've found a new job that I'm very excited about. I'll be making more money and will get to be the boss. Why couldn't you just say that?" Quentin asked. "D'you think I'm too weak to take it? Do you think lying made me feel better?" His voice grew louder. "Do you think after all this time I wouldn't be happy for you? Do you? Do you?" Quentin began to cry. "Fuck, isn't that what friends are for?"

Feeling ashamed, a loser, a clinical has-been that never was, I could barely face Quentin. Everything he said was true. I hadn't shown him any of the relief and pride I felt to be completing my internship and graduate training. I hadn't shown any of the pride and pleasure I felt anticipating a real job for which I'd be paid more than a pittance. Denying those truths had cast doubt over the truths I did express: my true sadness about leaving Quentin and my wish that we were just embarking on a therapy to last years and years. Quentin understandably didn't know what to believe

To make matters worse, by suggesting that everyone but me was ending his therapy—that it was mandated by the rules of the hospital, the requirements of my graduate program, the demands of the new clinic—I conveniently excused myself of all responsibility for leaving Quentin. In fact, the way I'd put it to him, I wasn't leaving him but was, against my will, being taken away from him by other forces and agencies over which I had neither control nor interest. It was bullshit, I had to admit. Maybe not a hundred percent pure, but bullshit nonetheless.

While my failure brought up useful material in Quentin's last week, I hadn't done him any favor. He'd had plenty to talk about and suffer without my adding insult to his injury. However, it did promote our talking even plainer and better. Taking ownership of my going away to advance my career and life allowed Quentin to share more of his anger at me for leaving, as well as to explore what growing up means, not just pessimistically, but optimistically. Most of all, it reinvigorated the trusting relationship we'd both come to rely on. After that consequential hour, Quentin knew that when I said he'd taught me much, I meant it.

These forced terminations carry certain limitations and responsibilities. If the time constraints are known—as they are for a
practicum student, intern, or fellow in training—the children and
their parents who enter into these relationships deserve to know
what they are getting into at the therapy's outset. Beyond the usual
tasks (discussed below) these terminations need to involve an added
appreciation for cases in which the child requires more therapy,
when she hasn't finished her work even though her therapist is
leaving.

> "I'm never doing therapy again." Twelve-year-old Tabitha, who
> perpetually drew pictures to show to me, covered her drawing so I
> couldn't see it.
>   "But there'll be other therapists you might like even more,"
> I sophomorically suggested, having reminded her of my ending the
> practicum the previous hour (with four to go).
>   "I never liked you, so that won't be very hard," Tabitha
> replied, smiling at her clever jab despite her hurt.

I, a graduate student at that time, recounted the session for my
supervisor; having overseen my work with this girl for the past eight
months, he knew the situation well. He recognized how much of
an achievement was the warm connection that Tabitha, a profoundly
neglected child, and I shared. Immediately, he gave me credit for
trying to do something decent, helping Tabitha give another therapist a try so that she might proceed with the work that was undone.

But his more patient ear heard and taught me otherwise.
"Why," he asked, "are you rushing to send her off?" Hurt by what
felt like an awful accusation, I began to protest my affection for her
and my upset that she had to move on to someone else. He cut me
off, though, questioning neither my intentions nor my caring. "You
feel so bad for abandoning her that you can't bear to hear her hurt
or see her bereft and alone. You want to find her a new parent so
as not to feel so rotten about leaving her."

Renewed by this insight, I was able to allow Tabitha most of our remaining few weeks together to process our terminating, which meant for her to get upset, complain, reject me, reject herself, and fall helpless and hopeless at my feet. Contrary to my earlier strategy, I brought up nothing about the promise of a second therapist or a future therapy. We instead wallowed in her present realization that I was leaving her stone-cold in a time of need.

> Midway through her next-to-last session, and to my astonishment, Tabitha casually mentioned that she wouldn't mind having a woman therapist next time around. This led to our comfortably discussing, in the final hour, Tabitha's spontaneous request that I help find her a new girl therapist who, she hoped, would be even better than me. I did. They hit it off and the treatment relationship worked out splendidly.

In other cases I've worked with (and supervised students who worked with) children and parents don't want to start again, at least not at that time. For some, the injury and loss is too great. Anticipating a new therapy and its burdens—getting to know each other, getting to trust each other, having to explain what feels like everything all over again—looms as too much and not worth the effort. Understandably, how hard it must be for a child who's deep in the midst of losing her therapist to look enthusiastically toward meeting a new one who, she knows too well, will likewise leave someday. To lay a guilt trip on them or overly warn of the hazards of not resuming treatment can instill resentments that may deter the family's ever coming back for help. For these children and parents our job is to let them leave with a good feeling for the specific work they have done and for the mental health profession in general, keeping the door open, so to speak.

Fortunately, as we progress in our careers we get to work through more complete treatments that are terminated, not out of third-party mandates or therapist life changes, but out of consideration for the child's needs. No longer relying on other agencies or forces to set the end limits of our therapies, we must assess for ourselves, along with the child and her parents, when she has done the work. What are the general indicators that tell us a child may be ready to end her therapy?

Symptoms, such as anxiety or depression, that have vanished or been reduced to tolerable levels. Problematic behaviors that have diminished or disappeared and perhaps been replaced by more adaptive and constructive ones. Greater capacities for bearing stress or negative emotions, such as sadness. Grieving that has gone its way. Developmentally stuck phases that have been surpassed. Trauma that has been mastered. Broader areas of functioning that are free from conflict. Improved reality testing and better judgment. Kinder consciences, lessened guilt, and more capacity to soothe oneself. Tolerance for ambivalence. Less ambivalence. More confidence and more resiliency. Less narcissistic vulnerability. Better relationships with family and friends. Improved capacities to play, work (mostly in school), and love. More trust and less mistrust. Greater self-control, less inhibition, and more expansive self-expression. Less distractibility. More openness to learning. Fewer headaches or other bodily stresses. Coming to terms with a limitation, such as a learning disability, and growing able and willing to use coping strategies and take constructive assistance that can help compensate. More independence. More dependence. Better separation. More attachment. Assertiveness. Compliance. A capacity to take pride and joy in accomplishments and in life. We may define changes in terms of fancy psychological concepts of substance: ego functioning, object relatedness, mastery of impulses, and evolution of self. Or we may more vividly notice a tense body that is relaxed, a sullen face that now smiles.

This abbreviated list of possible criteria speaks mostly to the wide range of issues for which children are brought to therapy. Which ones apply to a particular patient obviously involves our, the child's, and her parents' judgment. Although we may think the child capable of growing much braver and no longer susceptible to the pervasive anguish she now feels, her parents may feel that her being able to function at school and home is the mark of success. Our own capacity to see the child in her fullest glory in the context of both her therapy and the facts of her life (i.e., how she is doing on the outside) will make an assessment a doable thing, even if it involves some negotiating among the three players—child, parent, and therapist. Because we see the child each week, we also can be a bit blind to her changes. Occasionally taking a step back and contemplating these criteria, especially in relation to the child's therapeutic goals, facilitates our keeping ample track of the therapy's course, of where it is going and where it might end up.

While some children may feel sad and insecure about leaving therapy, a majority welcome the news of their readiness to do so as a sign of their success, of their having grown and being given the official sticker attesting to their psychic well-being, health, and strength. Although a fifty-minute hour doesn't take up much of a child's week, children frequently feel as if their schedule is being enormously freed up. "I'll have so much more time to play, hang out, do nothing . . ." their comments seem to convey.

As a rule, parents no less generally welcome the therapist's judgment that termination is appropriate. However much they support and appreciate our work with their child, being told that their child is in good shape can feel wonderful. That their busy schedules will be relieved of an hour or two just adds icing to the cake, as does the fact that a monthly bill won't be coming anymore. They may wonder whether this is too good to be true, harboring loving apprehension that their child's suffering or bad behaviors will return. But all in all, the decision to terminate a therapy that has come successfully to a natural conclusion is received with optimism and satisfaction.

Once all agree that terminating makes sense—because so much has been accomplished or because of diminishing returns—the issue of timing is faced. For children who've remained somewhat detached from therapy or who continue to have great difficulty knowing what they think and feel, children who use therapy less in terms of the relationship and more to practically solve problems in their lives, I sometimes agree with the parents' suggestion to phase therapy out slowly and less intensely, going to biweekly meetings then perhaps monthly sessions for a short while. These children will not, I know, make good psychological use of saying goodbye. They need something different; they need to know that I am still there for support. In the way that a child likes to know his mother is watching him play ball from the kitchen (though never seeking her out), these children want to know that I am not disappearing. Their termination is more of a "see you for now" (until you decide you wish to see me) than a therapeutic exploitation of finality.

In pacing a termination I tend to ask for at least a week for every three months of therapy, with a minimum (when possible) of six weeks for even a single year's work. A little longer is always better because it just gives us that much more time to work. For children who've attached firmly to me and the treatment and who can process their experiences with some agility, I suggest keeping the same weekly schedule right to the end. The sameness of routine—in terms of time and frequency—maintains the momentum that has carried the therapy up to that moment. To ease up on the schedule risks deflating the therapeutic tension, surrendering the value of the concluding work. Letting up can also give the wrong impression that we are deinvesting in the child, giving her permission to do the same.

> Pam looked a bit puzzled. We'd been discussing her irritation with a friend who had treated her with a superior air, a rather typical subject for this third year of a most thriving treatment.
>
> "What is it?" I asked.
>
> "Aren't we supposed to begin terminating today?" she asked.
>
> "We have been," I replied.
>
> "But," she looked around the office, "everything's the same. Same time. Same office. Same toys. Same you. Same me. You mean we do the same old thing right to the end?"

I nodded that indeed that was exactly what we would be doing. "Good," she replied. "I was afraid I was doing something wrong."

While termination can do more, as we will discuss, the bottom line of a good ending is to continue to provide the basic ingredients—empathy, keen listening, structure, boundaries, presence, confronting, and so on—allowing for the child's continued therapy as it is. Just because we're stopping doesn't mean that's the only subject we discuss. On the contrary, keeping the same steady therapeutic ax to the grindstone, in addition to offering children more time for productive work on their issues, helps them discover that their self-examination has been to a large degree a self-directed process. Proceeding with their therapy under the stress of our impending separation demonstrates to children that they can do the self-analysis and problem solving of therapy by themselves, or with others, as they go out on their own and for the rest of their lives.

Of course, the burden of working even as they anticipate our stopping is an essential one. Aware of the upcoming loss, children can grow apathetic or discouraged about their lives, fearful that they can't make it alone or simply feeling as if the meaning of their life and its efforts will vanish.

Marcus had made impressive strides in his hard-fought treatment. Teetering on the edge of delinquency, he had become a good student, good athlete, class leader, responsible friend, loyal son, and reliable patient. The determination to terminate his therapy had exhilarated him. He realized how far he'd come but he much appreciated his parents' and my vote of confidence in his growth.

Marcus began the termination process apparently pleased and looking forward to being done with treatment. With a few weeks to go, however, his life began to fall apart. He got detentions in school for coming late and unprepared to class, then got detentions on detentions for not showing up for those after-school punishments. At home he verbally assaulted his parents when they confronted his problems at school and threw tantrums when almost anything didn't go as he wished. Marcus skipped basketball practice and even began to smoke cigarettes, something he hadn't done for more than two years.

Although neither his parents nor the school were terribly thrown by this backslide—I'd warned them of the possibility at the time we'd decided on terminating—Marcus was. "See?" he said, having listed current difficulties, mostly misbehaviors. "The therapy didn't work. You were wrong, I'm in worse shape than when I came."

I smiled to myself, recalling the boy who, then truly at great risk, had first come to me. That boy took a year before he'd been able to acknowledge that his life was anything less than perfect.

"I'm not ready to stop therapy. I'm at great risk," he continued.

"Great risk for what?" I asked, reassured, not troubled, by what I was hearing. For children at risk tend not to discuss their risk in this manner, nor do they as a rule want or think they need the help of therapy.

"I don't know," Marcus said, tripped by my actually asking. "Everything."

I looked Marcus in the eye. "There's only one thing you're at risk for, and it's not failing school, or getting into trouble, or using drugs, or any of the other stuff you've mentioned. And I think you know what that is."

"What is it?" Marcus asked, having lost the bluster of his argument, appearing to both want and not want the answer.

"Missing me."

Several minutes of silence passed before Marcus spoke. "It seems kind of unfair that just when you're doing really good you lose the thing that helped you get there."

"You're right," I agreed. "It is unfair."

His not-so-unconscious wish to prove that he still needed me and therapy having been brought to the light of day, Marcus instantaneously regrouped and left therapy walking tall and straight.

Under the stress of termination, symptoms and old behaviors commonly return or intensify. They can be in the service of solic-

iting the therapist's help and concern (as were Marcus') or they can
have other, infinitely varied and unique meanings related to the
child's previous ways of coping with loss. In a therapy that has proceeded well and coherently, these temporary regressions need not
overly worry us.

> For months, actually since we began, Seth had pleaded not to have
> to come to treatment. He originally came with a myriad of
> symptoms that included stomachaches, high anxiety, school phobia,
> inhibition, skin rashes that broke out under stress, and constant
> irritability—most of which had subsided dramatically. Now his wish
> was coming true; he could really quit.
>
> Like Marcus, Seth was elated. "Now I can play with friends,"
> he speculated. "And watch television. And work on my go-cart.
> Bike ride, roller blade, swim, and skate. And just hang out, too."
> Seth had what sounded to be hundreds of hours of new activity
> slated to fill in the one free hour a week he was gaining (a sign, I
> hadn't yet realized, of the enormous void he was anticipating).
>
> But a couple of weeks following our joint decision to terminate
> Seth grew more anxious. He had to leave school because of nausea
> and stomach pains, and resisted going back. He grew clingy and
> refused to leave his mother for a dentist's appointment and a soccer
> practice. A friend's birthday party panicked him enough to stay
> home; most obvious of all, he broke out in hives over most of his
> body.
>
> Seth's regression disturbed his parents. Their fear (a near
> universal one for child patients and their parents) that his gains had
> been transitory or even illusory appeared to be coming to true.
> "Maybe he shouldn't stop," they wondered aloud. "Maybe therapy's
> never worked, or maybe he needs it forever," they added, the
> ambivalence of their doubt so wonderfully expressed in these bipolar
> alternatives. "Can't you do something?"
>
> Completely appreciating their distress, I knew what had to
> be done. Knowing that we'd made the determination to end therapy
> thoughtfully and slowly, and that it was a good decision, I reminded
> myself of the need to stay steady in the wake of this regression.

"Send Seth to school," I recommended matter-of-factly. "Don't pamper or medicate his bodily complaints. And he doesn't need to see a doctor." For he'd been evaluated thoroughly for all of his symptoms. "Basically, keep doing all of the good things you've learned to do over the past years of our work together."

"You mean the structure and the limits?" his mother asked. "But he seems so vulnerable right now."

I agreed that he was, stressing that the same reliable consistency was needed now, perhaps more than ever.

Likewise, I fended off my temptation to coddle Seth in a way I never had. Feeling bad that he would no longer have me, I felt a need to be more available, more active, more helpful, more supportive, more reassuring, more of everything. After all, in a short few weeks he wouldn't have me at all. But I knew better. To try and pour years of me into a handful of sessions might have alleviated my needs, but it would have harshly ignored and prolonged Seth's. Like a mother who feels guilt-ridden about her soon-to-be-born second child, who seductively invites her first child to regress, to be more of the baby, I would be setting Seth up for a certain fall if I gave him more and more just as I was about to be there not at all.

Enlightened by this self-counseling, I held back, making space for Seth to fend more for himself. "You're not helping me!" he exclaimed. "You're no good anymore," he became convinced. "I don't even know why I ever liked you."

Under my watchful if reserved eye, Seth floundered in his misery until ultimately, through his tears and gasps, he expressed his rage that I would be leaving him. I didn't mention that it was actually he who would be leaving me; that was irrelevant for now. Seth had it right. He would have to manage much of his hurt, and pleasure, and life, by himself.

Just as we had judged, Seth was indeed ready and capable of doing so. His cascade of old troubles came and went, a last hurrah for his more infantile means of coping that, however maladaptive and painful, had been precious to him. To give up old symptoms and behaviors meant to give up what was before, to put the past where it belonged—in the past.

Those regressions of termination, as well the more conscious reflecting that takes place, can allow for a remembering of what has gone before. In these final hours children will recall the states in which they began therapy, often pondering where they would have been had it not been for therapy, and reviewing their gains. They may pine nostalgically for what was, as well as look forward to the growth and life that lies ahead. Occasionally a child will make a book of therapy memories or some other concrete creation by which to document our time together. More commonly children will find themselves, perhaps quite unknowingly, revisiting old games, old activities, and old play that we shared, especially early on in the therapy.

Of course, the mother of all issues that terminating evokes is the obvious: the child's leaving of us and all that we've supplied—our holding, accepting, admiring, interest, patience, and belief that she holds the key, potential, and responsibility to overcome and grow.

Sara wanted to be a good girl, but she notoriously gave people a different impression. She was a child whose energy level could rival that of any nuclear particle, whose best intentions seemed always to go astray. Distractible and quite active, she was ever unwittingly creating mishaps with her fidgeting hands and feet, body parts that constantly sought stimulation, boundaries, and contact with others. Her constant questions and requests, then demands, for attention drained her much quieter and reserved parents.

Her complexity of personality and ego made her no less curious and challenging in school. A very bright child who could also act dumb when she chose, Sara worked hard for and was loved by some teachers. She could do little, or less, for other teachers, who came close to disdaining her. A magnetic personality who tended to attract or repel others, Sara left few people feeling indifferent toward her.

When she had entered therapy she was being followed closely by an eminent child psychiatrist and was on a medication that her parents judged to be helping with her concentration and impulsivity.

Yet both the parents and the psychiatrist felt there was more to her story. Psychological testing conducted before meeting me showed a proneness to depression, low self-esteem, lack of confidence in her ability to manage herself, and an exquisite vulnerability to narcissistic injury.

From our initial handshake Sara and I became fast allies in her self-exploration. Unfortunately, the task was to be much more arduous and trying than Sara anticipated. For months Sara would come to me, complaining of the gross mistreatment that she felt much of the world gave her. When secure in a therapeutic environment distinguished by patience, empathy, and nonintrusion, Sara was able to talk with increasing openness about the barbs and arrows of life that seemed to hit and bury in her skin. For the first time in her life, her parents reported, she could admit to the unhappiness that others could see in her. That she might be contributing to any of her difficulties, however, was not even a remote consideration.

When Sara and I butted heads (which wasn't often, for I was one of the good guys she worked hard to please), she tried to sidestep the issue, upping her attempt to charm and distract me. But one day, many months into treatment, Sara couldn't find enough space to run around a problem we shared. Cleaning up the office by wildly throwing toys backwards over her head at the toy box, she hit a framed picture with a small wooden block. We both knew what the cracking sound was before we even checked.

"I didn't mean it. Really, I didn't. I'm sorry. I'll pay for it." Sara apologized a mile a minute. "I wasn't trying to break the glass. I swear I wasn't."

Despite the therapist's proclivity to doubt what one protesteth so much, I did believe Sara. And that is where our work took hold. Rather than rush to accept Sara's apology, thereby rushing past this incident, I stayed silent, allowing Sara to flail.

"I don't know what gets into me," she bemoaned aloud. "I'm always screwing up. No matter what I try to do, it turns out bad. I tried to make my dad a gift for Father's Day, and I ended up getting glue all over his desk. He was furious and told me he'd rather I didn't make him gifts." Talking at the speed of light, Sara poured out her long-aching heart of the many assorted ways she'd made a mess of things. In between each avalanche of revelation she'd cry and cry.

That momentous occasion led to Sara's being able to examine, therapeutic molecule by molecule, the erratic and troubling incidents that pervaded her life. "Mrs. Collins hates me," she'd say, only to follow my empathic understanding for how bad that must feel with admissions as to what she'd done to get the teacher's goat. In her tedious and tortuous reconstruction, Sara began making distinctions between the *can't* and the *won't* of her trials and tribulations. Acknowledging more the frustration for times when she couldn't control herself and her actions led her to recognize the more-numerous-than-she'd-reckoned times when she could. Gaining the capacity to slow herself down, to contemplate and analyze the things she would do and what would happen to her as a result, brought insights into unconscious motivations for some of her action.

"My father thinks it's my ADD that makes me kick the back of his car seat," she decided. "But I really want to annoy him 'cause he thinks my sister's so much better." She similarly deciphered her not passing in homework she'd done ("No one's going to tell me what to do or when to do it") and her insulting of peers ("They all think they're so much better than I am") as well as many other facets of her attitude and behavior. While seeing more of the thoughts and feelings that went into her difficulties, she also came to better terms with her neurological susceptibility to distractibility and impulsivity. "I wish I was calm like a lake," she would sigh.

Her work progressed much further than any of us would have predicted, and the day came when Sara and her parents broached the question of termination. With apparent glee Sara looked at my calendar with me, deciding, with my approval, that we should meet for eight more weeks.

Sara used that time well. She kept analyzing the little pieces of life that pricked her skin and threatened her much stabilized ego. She worked actively on developing strategies to help her help herself, extrapolating the functions of myself to herself. For example, she decided that she could listen to herself carefully, just as I would do, before criticizing herself for something that went wrong. But in spite of all this able and worthy work that prepared for her terminating, Sara, in the first seven of our remaining eight hours, made no direct mention of our coming end.

It was not until the final hour that Sara made those sentiments known more fully. She had walked into the office behind my back while I was sitting at my desk.

"I'm sorry," I began to speak while putting my pencil down and closing up my scheduling book, "I was just mak . . ." Sara burst into tears.

"What is it, Sara?" I queried, knowing she was sad about our ending, but not knowing what specifically had precipitated her distress. She pointed to the book.

"This?" I asked, holding the book up, perplexed.

"Someone," she began to speak, but her emotions choked her. Minutes later, she explained. "Someone else is coming to see you next week." Again she broke down. "We're really stopping, aren't we?"

"Yes, we are, Sara. We are."

The feelings that had propelled the fine work she'd been able to do throughout the termination phase were held in this small packet and could wait no longer to be freed. Seeing me make note of another child's therapy hour had been too much reality to deny. The end had come.

Termination, in its fullest and richest sense, awakens children's deepest fears of separation, loss, and abandonment. For some, termination can resemble a psychic approximation of death, giving the anguishing impression that they are losing someone most dear to them . . . forever. It is a metaphor for the goodbye of goodbyes; children confront the longings that they most cherish. In their hard work they have come to more realistic terms with who they and their loved ones are. They have likely surrendered unreachable ideals that have haunted and punished them for being less. Putting some of their past in its proper place they have grieved people, places, and things. Odd or trite as it may sound, they have even grieved for the selves they once fancied they could be and for the children they never will be again. And besides just giving up their longings for and fantasies of the therapists they imagined we might be, they must give up the real therapists who did nothing more and nothing less than be with them through it all.

From their very first step into our office we have worked ever hard to make children's contact with us a worthwhile one. For some children the play and talk of therapy comes easily and with pleasure, our presence a constant comfort and support. For others the kinship is much rougher, that same play and talk an onerous burden and source of humiliation and resentment. Whatever the course of our relationship, and however successful or frustrating the outcome, we strive to send children out from therapy able to take pride and joy in a job well done, and on footing surer than they came in on, with the promise of sustained growth and continuing progress as they return to a life without us.

References

Abbott, K. (1990). The use of play in the psychological preparation of preschool children undergoing cardiac surgery. *Issues in Comprehensive Pediatric Nursing* 13:265–277.

Bromfield, R. (1989). Psychodynamic play therapy with a high-functioning autistic child. *Psychoanalytic Psychology* 6:439–453.

———— (1997). *Playing for Real: Exploring the World of Play Therapy and the Inner Worlds of Children.* Northvale, NJ: Jason Aronson.

Diagnostic and Statistical Manual of Mental Disorders, Fourth Edition (DSM-IV) (1994). Washington, DC: American Psychiatric Association.

Ginott, H. (1959). The theory and practice of "therapeutic intervention" in child treatment. *Journal of Consulting Psychology* 23:160–166.

Linn, S. (1986). Puppet therapy with pediatric bone marrow transplant patients. *Journal of Pediatric Psychology* 11:37–46.

Merriam-Webster's Collegiate Dictionary, Tenth Edition (1993). Springfield, MA: Merriam-Webster.

Rambert, M. (1949). *Children in Conflict.* New York: International Universities Press.

Winnicott, D. (1945). Primitive emotional development. In *Through Pediatrics to Psycho-Analysis.* London: Hogarth.

———— (1951). Transitional objects and transitional phenomena. In *Through Paediatrics to Psycho-Analysis.* London: Hogarth.

Index

Intervention
  behavioral limits, 74
  change, 49–50
  education, 54
  empathy, 47–49
  insight, 50–52
  neutrality, 50
  transference, 52–54
  unwilling patients, 232

King, S., 167

Language, talking and querying,
    82–83, 88
Learning disabilities, games,
    116–117
Lego-type toys, 124
Limits. *See* Boundaries and limits
Linn, S., 104
Listening, first meetings, 11

Medical procedures, puppet and
    action figure play, 104
Medication, 253–263
  child, consultation with,
      156–257
  evaluation, 253–255
  hazards of, 260–263
  parents and, 255–256
  psychiatric referral,
      257–258
  therapeutic relationship,
      258–260
Missing items, artwork, 145
Mistrust, trust and, unwilling
    patients, 234–235
Moustakas, C., 43

Narcissism, first meetings, 15
Narcissistic injury, unwilling
    patients, 232–233
Narcissistic vulnerability, games,
    118–119
Neglect. *See* Abuse and neglect
Neurological assessment,
    evaluation, 26–27
Neutrality
  intervention, 50
  talking and querying, 81

Observation, evaluation, 25–26
Oedipal conflict, games, 118
Office, physical environment,
    first meetings, 9–11
Open-ended questions, talking
    and querying, 80

Pacing, puppet and action figure
    play, 106
Parent–child relationship
  artwork, 143, 145
  evaluation, 27–28
  feedback, 31–34
  respect for, first meetings, 13
Parents, 209–225
  alliance with, 210–211
  child therapy
    first meetings, 7, 15–16
    initiation of, 5–7
    listening to, 11, 12
  developmental factors, 216–
      217
  forced termination, 269
  gifts, 191–193
  guidance of, 224–225

dependency, 235–238
emotion and, 230–231
intervention, 232
narcissistic injury, 232–233
parents, 232, 241–242
resistance, 238–241

strategies for, 234
trust and mistrust, 234–235

Wild analysis, puppet and action
figure play, 108
Winnicott, D. W., 104

ABOUT THE AUTHOR

Richard Bromfield, Ph.D., is a graduate of Bowdoin College and the University of North Carolina at Chapel Hill. A faculty member of Harvard Medical School at the Massachusetts Mental Health Center, he writes about children, psychotherapy, and family life in both professional and popular periodicals. Author of *Playing for Real: Exploring the World of Play Therapy and the Inner Worlds of Children* and the forthcoming *Handle with Care: Understanding What Children Think, Feel, Say, Do (and Draw) in the Classroom*, he is a regular reviewer for *Psychoanalytic Psychology*. Dr. Bromfield has a private practice with children and adults in both Brookline and Hamilton, Massachusetts.